RIGHT PLACE
RIGHT TIME

THE INSIDE STORY OF
CLOUGH'S DERBY DAYS

RIGHT PLACE RIGHT TIME

THE INSIDE STORY OF CLOUGH'S DERBY DAYS

GEORGE EDWARDS

First published 2007
Reprinted 2008, 2014

The History Press
The Mill, Brimscombe Port,
Stroud, Gloucestershire, GL5 2QG
www.thehistorypress.co.uk

British Library Cataloguing in Publication Data.
A catalogue record for this book is available from the British Library.

ISBN 978 0 7524 4445 1

Printed and bound in Great Britain

CONTENTS

ABOUT THE AUTHOR

George Edwards joined the *Derby Evening Telegraph* as a trainee reporter when he was sixteen, three days after leaving Queen Elizabeth Grammar School, Ashbourne, and moved into the sports department in 1960 when he was just eighteen. By the age of twenty-three he was covering Derby County and three years later was appointed sports editor, filling both roles until 1973 when he returned to general news to become assistant editor. He subsequently moved to Swansea to become deputy editor and later editor of the *South Wales Evening Post*, from which he retired in the autumn of 2002.

He and his wife Rosalind, when not watching England play cricket at home and abroad, split their time between two former fishing villages, Mumbles in South Wales and Sabinillas in Southern Spain.

THE AUTHOR WOULD like to thank the *Derby Evening Telegraph* for supplying many of the images reproduced in this book.

PREFACE

Steve Bloomer, Hughie Gallacher, Jack Bowers, Raich Carter, Peter Doherty… Derby was always a football town, but never did football grab the emotions as it did during the club's greatest era, in which Brian Clough and Peter Taylor swept the club from obscurity to unimagined success. I was fortunate to work closely with football's most remarkable double act from the day they joined Derby County until the day they left. It is, I fear, almost impossible to capture completely the thrills of the journey from cautious optimism to almost permanent jubilation as Derby became awash with football fever created by the tidal wave that was Clough and Taylor, but I have done my best.

So much of journalism and newspaper life is down to fortune, good and bad, of being in the right place at the right time. Luck, in other words, and it was my good luck to be reporting Derby County matches during the club's greatest era.

That good fortune favoured me at other times, leading to encounters, some funny, some sad, with people as different as 'tired and emotional' Labour Party stalwart George Brown, comic genius Tommy Cooper, Olympic legend Jesse Owens and President Kennedy. On a more parochial level, Derby people who supported the club through its golden age will no doubt remember the eccentric street trader Mad Harry, Pigeon Percy, Sammy Ramsden and larger-than-life club owner Tommy Barnes.

I'm afraid I have indulged myself, too, briefly recalling schooldays, feeble attempts to make the grade as a sportsman and my early years as a young reporter, coping with heartbreaking death knocks, murder trials and failed attempts to claim as little as tuppence on expenses. There's also plenty of unashamed name dropping, but I hope you enjoy the book anyway.

George Edwards

PROLOGUE

There we were crammed into the boys' enclosure, or the kids' pen, as it was better known; a cynical concession to youngsters, holding probably no more than 100 or so, all shapes and sizes, and affording the worst possible view of the game from its position by the corner flag and slightly below the level of the pitch. This was the Baseball Ground on 18 August 1951, the first day of the season, and as a pint-sized youngster my excitement was tempered by frustration since I could see practically nothing. But it was thrilling all the same and I joined in for all I was worth when the cheerleader arrived, clad from head to toe in black and white, top hat included, and flourishing his heavy wooden rattle. He seemed to me incredibly old and he probably was, but we loved him, especially when he launched into his stirring call to action. 'Two, four, six, eight, who do we appreciate,' he bellowed. 'D–E–R–B–Y, DERBY' we all chorused before madly swinging our own rattles. Those wonderful implements made a marvellous noise but have, of course, long been banned from modern football grounds because they could be used as weapons of considerable destruction. It's a shame, but a sign of the times. Back then crowd trouble was unheard of. We just cheered or occasionally booed as did everybody else around the ground, young and old.

A few months earlier, towards the end of the previous season, persistent nagging paid off when I persuaded my aunt and uncle, who were Derby County season-ticket holders, to take me to my first game. They were to pick me up at two o'clock, but I was waiting on the pavement long before, peering anxiously up the road until my uncle's old Rover

ARC846 came round the corner. Even in those gently naïve days when there was an almost automatic assumption nothing unpleasant could happen I was considered too young and certainly too small to stand on my own, so I sat next to my aunt and uncle, looking around in something of a dream. Where had all these people come from? I started to count and after a minute or two confidently declared that as there were about eighty people near us so there must be at least 1,000 at the game. My uncle said he thought there were a few more and he was right, since records show the attendance was 16,788. The Rams beat Middlesbrough 6-0 and, though I did not realise it at that time, I had watched the great Wilf Mannion in action. Neither did I realise that this afternoon out was to shape my life. The Derby team that day included the youthful Albert Mays, a gifted all-round ball player who excelled at cricket and was an outstanding snooker player. A few seasons later I queued for his autograph. Not so many years after that I drank in his pub and took him to matches; later again, sadly not much later, I visited him in hospital where he was dying of lung cancer, at forty-four still a relatively young man.

But back in March 1951 I was just nine, a product of the war years and, like so many of my contemporaries, innocent, impressionable and unused to any of the trappings of even modest wealth, so there was further quickening of the pulse when my aunt and uncle took me home to their flat for tea after that first game. Not only did they have a car, a rarity in those days, but also a television, which was even rarer. Come the start of the new season I was still dependent on Uncle Ian to get me to the ground, but I was now standing on my own two feet, or rather tiptoes, in that cramped throng of youngsters in the kids' pen. This was how to spend a Saturday afternoon. The season flew by and I marvelled at the skills of Derby's diminutive outside right Reg Harrison, not to mention assorted opposing right-wingers, just about the only players I could see properly. Reg was a marvel, firing over perfect centres towards Jack Stamps, a huge man who even then was always described as an old-fashioned centre forward. Jack headed everything in at one end while centre half Ken Oliver, whose nickname 'Rubberneck' needs no explanation, headed everything away at the other. Who was to know that Jack would go blind in his fifties and Ken would die before his time from a brain-related disease? Those heavy leather balls had a lot to answer for.

I soon discovered the *Green'un*, the Saturday-night football paper produced by the *Derby Evening Telegraph*, so what I had not been able to see I could at least read about thanks to the expertise of sports reporter Eddie Giles, who seemed to me to have the best job in the world; not just watching football, but watching Derby County and being paid for it. I read Eddie avidly and some time later – I suppose I was about eleven – took the plunge and wrote perhaps the most important letter of my life. How did you get this job, Mr Giles? How could I get a similar job when I'm old enough? Do you have to work on weekdays as well? About a week later I received a reply; not a quickly dashed off typed note, but a long hand-written letter on Basildon Bond paper, running to several pages. I was overwhelmed and read the letter over and over again. Work hard on your English at school. Learn as much as you can about all sport, read as many newspapers as you can, in fact, read anything and everything. He told me how he had started in journalism and how he had worked his way up. He even told me of his own ambitions to work on a national newspaper. Well, English was the only subject I was any good at and I already read every newspaper and sports magazine I could lay my hands on. So there was hope.

'Hello Eddie, how are you?' It was perhaps fifteen years later and I was sitting in the Baseball Ground press box preparing to cover a game, when I overheard somebody behind me welcome a reporter I had not seen before. Instinctively I turned and asked him whether he was Eddie Giles. He was and we shook hands. He remembered my letter and we chatted over all that had happened in the intervening years, during which he had moved to the *Daily Telegraph* and I had graduated from the school desk to the sports desk. We had both achieved our ambitions and not surprisingly became great friends. Eddie set me off on a forty-four-year career in the regional press by the end of which I had achieved all my ambitions and more. Over the years I must have received scores, probably hundreds of letters from young people at school eager to become journalists. I cannot vouch for the quality of the advice I offered, but my replies were always long and detailed if not on Basildon Bond notepaper.

CHAPTER 1

STARTING OUT

It may be that not every small boy kicking a ball around just after the war wanted to be Stanley Matthews, but that was how it seemed. For the most part playgrounds were dominated by the best footballers and at my little primary school, on the outskirts of Derby, the best player was Peter Ekins, who became a pal when we were five-year-olds and has remained a great friend ever since. In his teens Pete played in the North *v.* South England Boys trial but got no further, probably because the system was hopelessly corrupt. The selectors – teachers all – inevitably looked after their own favourites, and nothing much changed for years afterwards, so while only a handful of those selected for the England schoolboy team made the grade, many overlooked for reasons of bias came good and enjoyed careers as professionals. St Peter's, Littleover, was not a great football school and despite the best efforts of Peter and our excellent centre forward Terry Hudson, we were regularly slaughtered by nearby Gayton Avenue School, for whom Chris Barker was particularly outstanding. A few years later Chris was bombarded by offers to turn professional – notably by West Ham United at the time Bobby Moore and Geoff Hurst were starting their careers – but for his own reasons turned them all down. These days the money would surely have been a sufficient lure and he would be a multi-millionaire living in some Cheshire mansion or a Virginia Water penthouse. Modest though we were on the football field, St Peter's was a good school, pupils doing as they were told and responding to the efforts of teachers who had no cause to worry about rebellious children or parents invading the classroom threatening to black their eye. My mother kept my school reports and they confirm that while I was an able pupil it was only English at which I consistently excelled. However, one year, when I was eight, my report was unusually good and thus presented a challenge for our headmaster Mr Whitehall, who liked to provide a sting for every tail. Faced with having to comment on a report littered with Excellent, V.G. and Outstanding Progress, his solution was to write at the foot of this success story 'Not very neat with ink', which was undoubtedly true at the time and would be just as true today. Summer holidays were blissful, especially when Derbyshire were playing cricket at the County Ground. Four or five of us, even at the age of nine or ten, were allowed to disappear all day, our parents presumably relying on safety in numbers. We always wanted Derbyshire to bowl so we could watch the great Les Jackson steaming in at one end with the cunning Cliff Gladwin at the other. Young though we were we could never understand why Jackson did not play for England, but then neither could others far older and wiser than we. Watching Derbyshire bat was never quite so much fun, so we would often pass the time playing our own games of cricket with a lemonade bottle and a ball of rolled up newspaper, cricket's version of jumpers for goalposts.

Politicians who talk these days about people existing at poverty level obviously have no clue about life for practically everybody in the late 1940s and early '50s, though there was a posher term for it then – post-war austerity. As Christmas approached my mother supplemented the family income by sitting in our little kitchen every evening plucking chickens for the local poulterer at 6*d* a time, which used to leave her fingers red and bleeding. Nobody had a television, so we all listened to the radio – *Riders of the Range* and *Dick Barton* in the week, *Billy Cotton's Band Show* and *Educating Archie* on Sundays along with the unmissable *Two-way Family Favourites*, in which messages and record requests were sent to and from service families abroad. 'Look Homeward, Angel' and 'I'll Be Home' seemed to be requested every week. Where today's youngsters have Saturday morning television, we had the cinema, in our case The Cavendish ('the Cavo'), where we paid sixpence to be entertained from ten o'clock until midday. First was the singsong, words up on the screen, 'We come along on Saturday morning, greeting everybody with a smile,' followed by assorted patriotic songs like 'Pack Up Your Troubles' and 'Old Father Thames', then came a cartoon, the weekly serial – perhaps *Dick Barton* or *Flash Gordon* – and finally the feature film, more often than not a western, but sometimes *Laurel* *and Hardy* or *Will Hay*. Sixpence made quite a hole in my two shillings pocket money, but it was great value. Like most Derby people we found enough money for a week in a caravan each summer. What excitement. A crowded platform at Derby's old Friargate Station and a comic to read on the seemingly endless journey to Skegness. There were no ranks of taxis at Skeggy. The wealthier went off to hotels in horse-drawn carriages while the rest of us sought out one of the horde of small boys, each waiting with a trolley, a set of pram wheels with a board attached to the top, pulled by a rope. The lads would pile suitcases on these ingenious devices and set off full pelt to guest houses and caravan parks with owners of all shapes, sizes and ages struggling along in pursuit. The days were all spent on the beach, my father, who away from the sports field never really saw the point of moving if the other option was to remain stationary, spending hours lazing around reading, at least until one day when he disappeared for ages, before joining us at lunchtime looking thoroughly fed up. It turned out he had lost a ten-shilling note and had spent all morning walking up and down the promenade looking for it, which was not surprising because it probably represented three nights' beer money. That same year the *Eagle* comic arranged what would now be called a road show, involving games on the beach and a race for children along the prom over a mile or so. As I had always liked running I decided to have a go and soon found myself bowling along the seafront fairly easily so I sped up a bit and came home first, winning a penknife, hardly the sort of prize they would be likely to hand out these days. An interest was sparked.

I was sorry to leave St Peter's, with its homeliness and security, but excited about the prospect of going to Queen Elizabeth Grammar School at Ashbourne, even though it was thirteen miles away and they didn't play football. I thought it would be just like Littleover but bigger, so was totally unprepared for the startling contrast. The distant unfriend-liness of the teachers in their caps and gowns initially left me baffled and depressed, on top of which there was the bus ride to and from school. Suddenly I was going out at about 7.40a.m., long before my father went to work, and getting in at the same time he did, but it was hardly *Tom Brown's Schooldays* and I grew to like and admire several of the teachers, especially our Latin master Peter Jennings, a remarkable man who had been terribly disfigured during the war. When I saw him on my first day I could not help but stare. He had, to all intents and purposes, a plastic head; no skin, no hair, no eyebrows, a tiny button nose and a thin almost lipless mouth. This was the man I had heard about even before I got to Ashbourne; this was the terrifying Peanut. Can there ever have been a crueller nickname? I never discovered exactly what happened, but apparently he was shot down and badly burned during the Battle of Britain when he was twenty and survived only after a series of operations. He was one of the first to have his face rebuilt by the legendary pioneer plastic surgeon Archibald McIndoe, but got on with his life once his treatment was over with what was obviously extraordinary courage. About ten years after I left school I took a call on the *Derby Telegraph* sports desk and a faintly familiar voice asked, 'Do you know who this is?' When I hesitated there was a chuckle. 'It's Peter Jennings, Peanut to you.' He wanted me to give a short talk to the boarders at Ashbourne, an invitation I was delighted to accept. It was wonderful to see him again, but I still could not bring myself to ask precisely what happened, nor to tell him how terrifying I first thought him. Our geography master, Jock Coates, who fought in the First World War, was much travelled and prefaced all his many anecdotes with the words 'when I was in Mesopotamia,' which, though we all knew it was coming, set off the gigglers among us. He was my house master and he and I got on quite well, especially in the afternoons, since it was well known that he spent the entire lunch break in the pub, doubtless telling people about Mesopotamia when he wasn't studying the racing pages. On one occasion, just before the start of afternoon lessons, I was reading something on the noticeboard when he swayed up to me, put an elbow on my shoulder and said unexpectedly loudly, 'George, I'm off at the end of the term. I can't stand this place any more,' before lurching off in the direction of the staffroom. This was extraordinary in more than one respect because it was unheard of for a boy to be called by his Christian name.

While I was distinctly up and down academically, usually more down than up, there was always the sport. I discovered I was a decent runner, breaking the school 440 yards record and captained the junior cricket and rugby teams, though I was neither big enough nor brave enough to make much of a rugby player. I developed a useful sidestep, usually to get out of the way of opponents bigger than me, which was most of them. The fact that Ashbourne was coeducational was also a distinct plus, probably not unconnected to my academic shortcomings.

Saturdays were wonderful. Early in the morning I would head for the railway station to meet my friends with a packet of sandwiches, my autograph book filled with pictures cut from newspapers and football magazines and another book in which to jot down train numbers. What value we got for our penny platform ticket. The train-spotting bit was easy. We knew what trains were due and when, so dashed from platform to platform, cheering or groaning depending on what loco steamed in. Train-spotters later became figures of fun, all anoraks, lapel badges and binoculars, but I suspect many of us learned far more about the geography of England collecting train numbers than we ever did at school. Collecting autographs was much more of a challenge. Many football teams travelled by train in those days and chances were they would pass through Derby. Thus, for instance, if Manchester United were playing at Arsenal, we could expect them to arrive around mid-morning and we knew which train to ambush. The knack was to watch each carriage closely as the train pulled in until we spotted the ones with reserved stickers pasted on the windows. Then off we ran, leaping on to the train if we knew it was to stop for a few minutes and bursting into the appropriate compartment where the players were usually more than happy to sign the books we thrust at them. If the train was to make only a brief stop then we took a chance and pushed our books through the windows while our heroes signed and it always worked – always until the day a train pulled away with my book still in the clutches of somebody I had probably never heard of. I had risked my precious collection just to get the signatures of a few players from Darlington and it had gone, leaving me in despair. I was, however, rewarded for having the good sense to write my name and address inside the cover. A few days later I returned from school to find a parcel containing my book, a handful of programmes and a short letter from Ken Furphy, one of the Darlington players. I followed his career closely from that day. From the station it was on to the Baseball Ground to watch the match, first team or reserves, the second-team games often providing a better chance to collect prestigious autographs, because Derby were then in the old Third Division North while the Reserves might be playing their counterparts from a First Division club, who would sometimes field famous players dropped or coming back from injury. We cycled everywhere, which meant leaving our bikes for safe keeping down the entry of any of the tiny terraced houses close to the ground. This cost us tuppence, which even in those days seemed good value. Add the cost of the platform ticket and we had quite a day out for a fraction more than a penny in today's money.

During my fourth year at Ashbourne we were visited by a careers officer who looked a little startled when I told him I hoped to be a sports writer and report on Derby County matches. I don't think he really knew what to say but his advice, to take any job on the paper which might be offered, was sound and his visit prompted me to approach the *Derby Evening Telegraph* again. Eddie Giles had by then moved on, so I wrote to Charles Forrest, the editor, and told him of my ambitions. About two weeks later I sat before him in a huge panelled office, suddenly revisited by the chronic stammer that had afflicted me as a small boy. I was certain my inarticulate mumbling had scuppered me, but consoled that I had been asked to submit a film review, a sports report and an essay outlining why I wanted to be a journalist. These I duly produced and shortly afterwards a letter arrived. Charles Forrest had been sufficiently impressed by my efforts to pass them on to his chief sub-editor Bob Randall. He too had liked them and, said the editor, felt I was worth a chance when I left school, provided, of course, I passed the eight GCE O-level examinations I was sitting. That was the autumn of 1957. In October 2002, forty-five years later, Bob Randall and his wife Audrey, Bob then nearing eighty, made the long journey from their home to East Anglia to West Wales for my retirement lunch. Thankfully nobody had ever asked me about the O-level results.

CHAPTER 2

SUNFLOWERS, DEATH KNOCKS AND SOME GREAT RUNNERS

Whether 1958 was a good year for sunflowers I have no idea, but when Norman Peace, the news editor, learned a reader had grown a particularly handsome specimen he thought it important enough to dispatch a reporter and photographer to investigate. An hour into my first day I was sent along to observe, thus three of us turned up at the reader's house where we gazed respectfully at the bloom in question. This was not terribly exciting and neither was I overwhelmed by the financial rewards because at the end of my first week I went home with £3, half of which I gave to my mother, leaving me just about enough for bus fares and a snack at lunchtime. Not that I was alone in struggling to make ends meet. I remember one of the reporters, asked whether he was going for a drink after work, saying he was stopping in for two or three weeks because he was saving up for a shirt. This shortage of money hit me particularly hard one week. The paper ran a face-in-the-crowd competition, which involved publishing a picture of a section of the Baseball Ground terracing on match day with the head of one fan circled. That person had only to present himself at the *Telegraph* office to earn 10s 6d, and it was my job to check the winner and hand over the money. It was a simple enough procedure which involved taking the photograph to the front counter, inspecting the claimant as closely as seemed polite and, when satisfied, handing over the money. This presented no problem until one Saturday when, shortly after I had returned to the newsroom, a second man arrived at the office who, I quickly realised, was undoubtedly the person in the picture. In something of a panic I fled back upstairs, where

Norman Peace was unperturbed and duly produced a further 10s 6d. So that was that, I thought, until a few minutes later I found myself sent to retrieve the money from the original 'winner'. A little reluctantly off I went, but as I approached the man's house I saw him strolling along carrying what looked suspiciously like a large box of chocolates, at which point my nerve went completely. I cycled quickly past, head down, and went back to the office with no option but to hand over ten and six of my own money. Luckily I had been paid the day before.

The sports department was a closed shop, at least until I was sent to Burton-on-Trent with Wilf Shaw, the paper's cricket writer, for a game against Hampshire. Burton hosted just one game a year and the *Telegraph* did not have a telephone in the press box, so my job was to run to the nearest call box every half-hour or so and phone Wilf's report back to the office. This was more like it and it was my good luck that the game was one of the most remarkable in the county's history. The wicket was not really up to first-class standard and in no time at all Derbyshire were all out for just 74, but that was nothing compared with what was to come, because the great Les Jackson was pawing the ground. Hampshire, at one point 11 for 8, were bowled out for 23 runs in 16.4 overs, Jackson taking 5 for 10 and we had not even reached tea. The game was all over well before lunch the next day, Derbyshire reaching 107 in their second innings, then bowling Hampshire out for 55, the entire match lasting only 114 overs. But running copy was not always such fun. Certain things stick in the mind and seeing a man sentenced to death is certainly one of them. Sent to Nottingham Assizes to phone back our reporter's account of a murder trial, I found the pomp and procedure, the cross-examinations and the skills of the barristers fascinating, but was not prepared for the conclusion, when the man in the dock, who had killed his grandmother by stabbing her in the stomach with a poker, was found guilty and duly sentenced. He did not hang, of course, because hanging was almost at an end in the late 1950s, but I can still see him standing upright, staring blankly ahead as his sentenced was pronounced. Any passing fancy I might have had that capital punishment was justified vanished forever that day. Neither did I enjoy Monday mornings, because part of any youngster's training was to tackle the dreaded death knock. It seemed that every weekend somebody, usually a child, was killed in a road accident and inevitably it was my job to interview the families. In my case this meant turning up at the house, knocking quietly on the door and hoping nobody was in, but usually there was and I found myself talking to grief-stricken parents. These days this is rightly regarded as gross intrusion of privacy, but not back then. Indeed, so far as I know, nobody ever complained, not even when I asked to borrow a photograph. One or other of the parents, perhaps still in some sort of trance, would take a framed picture of the child from the mantelpiece or top of the television and hand it to me, usually with a politely plaintive request to have it returned if possible. On one occasion a toddler was run over on the Mackworth Estate just outside Derby and again it was my job to find out exactly what had happened. A red-eyed, unshaven father opened the door, ushered me in and I sat blinking hard and swallowing even harder as he told me he had been in the garden when he caught sight of his three-year-old daughter on the other side of the road. Without thinking he had shouted to her to come back and she had looked across at him, reacted instinctively and run straight under the wheels of a bus. So not only had he seen his daughter die, he thought it his fault. I cycled back to the office determined to tell the news desk that I had had enough of death knocks, but of course I could not. Sixteen-year-old reporters all over the country were doing the same thing, no doubt feeling just as unhappy about it. A little while later I attended my first inquest, tagging along with a senior reporter, and by coincidence it was into the death of the same little girl. The bus driver, a tiny West Indian, who was entirely blameless, sobbed uncontrollably throughout and so did the father. This was not what I had in mind when I wrote to Eddie Giles and neither was it on the occasion the paper heard from a contact that a well-known showjumper had died after being thrown from her horse. Off I went, this time to the home of the woman's sister, a regular contributor to the paper. If I thought she was bearing up remarkably well this was because nobody had told her the news, so when I asked for a few details about her sister, she said 'Yes, of course, what's she been up to now?' Faced with the prospect of explaining that her sister was dead I muttered something about not being sure and that I had simply been told to ask for some career details and quickly made my escape. These days, thanks to all the procedures and protocols in place, such a thing could not happen. But it was not all doom and gloom, in fact, far from it. I studied the senior reporters with a mixture of admiration and astonishment, because things that would be unthinkable these days were run-of-the-mill back them. Most reporters were talented and conscientious, but some just drifted from one day to the next in an alcoholic haze. Joan Harris, a hell-raiser in the Oliver Reed class, could write superbly, but only when she could focus on her typewriter. One day she was scheduled to interview the film star Eva Bartok, then go to the Council House where a group of leading local business women were being entertained. The interview must have been spectacularly boozy, because Joan arrived at the Mayor's Parlour meeting mid-afternoon carrying a glass of beer she had presumably brought from the nearby White Horse pub and announced loudly 'that Eva Bartok is a f__g cow' before sliding down the wall until she was sitting on the floor, glass still in hand. It may well have been Joan who was responsible for another bizarre episode when some late-comer to the office one evening, instead of writing their full name in the register at the staff entrance, simply wrote 'balls' in capital letters. This caused a serious stir and prompted the hierarchy to demand that every reporter provide a specimen of their handwriting so the culprit could be identi-fied. Back then, of course, it was unthinkable to ask people to write 'balls', so we were all asked to write 'football's a great game'. As they say these days, you couldn't make it up.

I waited impatiently for the chance to report a football match and that chance came when I was dispatched to the wilds to report South Normanton Miners Welfare against Cresswell Colliery in the old Central Alliance. A bus to Alfreton, another to South Normanton and I was there, all geared up with my instructions – teams before the start, 100 words at half-time, scorers and score at the end. I covered a few more games at South Normanton before being posted to Belper, a little town eight miles from Derby. I was to go on the bus each morning, pick up what news I could and come back in the afternoon. And yes, I could cover Belper Town matches every Saturday. I suspect I did not pick up many news stories, but my coverage of Belper Town was comprehensive, because I spent most mornings sitting in the little front room of club secretary Norman Mellor drinking tea and talking football. If the players thought I was a little young, at seventeen, to be passing judgements on their efforts they never said so and neither did Norman, who was prob-ably just pleased his club was suddenly getting so much publicity. Fast forward to the 2002/03 season and I revisited Belper's Christ Church Meadows Ground. Gone was the rickety old fencing and in its place a fine stand and clubhouse. I went as soon as I could to the old photos on the wall and there was the team of 1959/60 with Norman Mellor and his lads gazing down at me, Norman in his baggy suit and trilby, the players in even baggier shorts.

I picked up snippets of news, reported courts and council meetings and called at the police station every morning where the desk sergeant was happy for me to look at his daily record of events. I also spent hours covering tedious planning appeals and was sitting in one such meeting when I heard the siren of a fire engine as it raced past. Just another chimney fire, I thought and stayed until the meeting finished a couple of hours later, but it was not a chimney fire. An old mill building had collapsed while being knocked down by a team of demolition workers and some of the men were trapped. By the time I arrived at the scene around 100 rescuers were desperately trying to clear the debris, watched by national newspaper reporters from all over the north of England and all this time I had been listening to somebody making a case for having his bungalow extended. Thankfully the *Telegraph* had sent two experienced members of staff so when I saw a crushed wheelbarrow carefully pulled from under 2,000 tons of rubble and realised a mangled body could be next, I slipped away. Thus I did not write any of the following day's story, but I did spend two days going to the homes of the four who died (miraculously it was only four) requesting photographs and biographical details. If I learned a lesson from that experience, I learned a lot more from Belper's MP George Brown, one-time Foreign Secretary and deputy leader of the Labour Party, renowned for his volatile temperament and liking for anything alcoholic. George, for whom the term 'tired and emotional' was later created, held a surgery for his constituents in the town once a fortnight so I turned up to see if any interesting issues had arisen. From time to time we would adjourn to the The Lion, where I would sip orange squash and George (Mr Brown to me then, of course) usually demolished the best part of a bottle of gin. He would then give me a lift back to Derby in his huge Humber car, covering the eight miles, much of it subject to a 30mph speed limit, in well under a quarter of an hour. He talked nothing but politics, something about which I knew nothing, but other than fearing for my life as he swung his car round the many tight bends on the A6, I loved every minute of it. He had charisma on a scale I had never previously encountered.

A five-and-a-half day week meant I had given up hope of playing football. I worked every Saturday and back then local authorities did not allow pitches to be used on a Sunday, but there was, I remembered, the

Derby Wednesday League, created especially for Saturday workers and as Wednesday was my half-day, I signed on for Derby Co-op. We weren't very good, especially compared with the Borough Police and the aptly-named Derby Butchers, but win or lose we never failed to be amused by the advice of our team manager, an enthusiastic original thinker from the soft furnishings department. In the first half of one game our centre forward sent a series of shots ballooning over the bar, prompting the manager to devise a most unlikely solution. 'You keep putting it over the top, Albert,' he said at half-time. 'Try shooting from further out and the ball should drop just underneath the bar.' Curiously this didn't seem to work. My love of athletics endured and somehow, thanks to cycling to and from work and surviving largely on Mars Bars, I saved enough to pay for a trip to the 1960 Olympic Games in Rome with an old school friend, Robin Blunt, and Jerry Keily, whose elder brother Arthur was running in the marathon. Eighteen nights in a small hotel, rail travel each way and tickets for every day's athletics: total cost £82. Amazing… but throw in £20 spending money and it was the equivalent of almost six months' pay. Security was almost non-existent, so we jumped on the competitors' buses heading back to the Olympic village, then wandered into one of the many dining areas and ate as much as we could alongside the likes of Herb Elliott and Peter Snell. Strolling round one day I spotted a slightly podgy, balding man leaning against a wall enjoying the sun, whose face I thought looked familiar. I took a chance, told him my name and asked whether he would sign my autograph book. I thanked him as he did so and glanced down to read 'Good luck, George, from Jesse Owens'. On another occasion, keen to see Derby weightlifter Louis Martin compete (he won a bronze), Jerry, Robin and I strolled in through the competitors' entrance despite weighing not much more than twenty stone between the three of us. A confident smile at the man on the door, a pat on his shoulder and through we went. Jerry Keily, a brilliant footballer, whose career with Sunderland was ruined by a knee injury, took up running and when I last saw him he was complaining that he had been forced to cut back on his training because his dodgy knee was playing up. He was eighty-two at the time, so perhaps this was understandable. Just a few weeks before the Games, I had been called to see the editor, which was odd because Charles Forrest was rarely seen, so I suppose I was apprehensive when I tapped on his door, but CF, though a remote figure, was not frightening. He waved me in, sat me down where I had sat as a fifteen-year-old not long before, and told me one of the sports reporters was leaving. If I wished I could go into the sports department but it would be for a three-week trial period. Would I like to do so? I said I would. After three weeks I heard nothing and nobody in the sports department ever mentioned a trial period so there I stayed.

The sports editor was Cec Grounsell, the only man I have met who has forgotten how to type. This happened, so he said, during the war which naturally enough left me wondering why none of his contemporaries had been similarly afflicted. Cec, who wrote under the name of Mark Eaton, occasionally offered me some very odd advice. When I wrote in a match report that a team had 'held their own' in the second half he told me not to use the expression because holding your own was what you did when you went to the gents. The four-man department was helped from time to time by an Oxford University student, Gerald Mortimer, who appeared during holiday times and regarded both Grounsell and his deputy Wilf Shaw with an amused tolerance while I think they found his slightly superior undergraduate manner a little daunting. After Oxford Gerald went into teaching until, after a chance meeting several years later, I persuaded him to make a career change and move into journalism. He took a drop in pay to do so and went on to report Derby County games for more than thirty years, by far the longest stint of any of us.

Still the running nagged away. At that time Derby and County Athletic Club had by far the best cross-country and road-running team in the country. The Keily brothers, Arthur, Joe, Mike and Dominic, Mike Bullivant and Peter Wilkinson were British internationals and several more of the team ran for England. The Keilys were an extraordinary family of Irish extraction, born and raised – all ten children – in a tiny terraced house near the railway station in Trinity Street, which had an outside lavatory and no bathroom, which meant everybody washed in the kitchen sink. Keily senior had been killed at Dunkirk and little Annie Keily brought up the children on her own, apparently with a teapot permanently attached to her right arm. I often called round at lunchtime when the little parlour was usually crammed with up to a dozen people and running was the only topic. Arthur, the eldest, whose job involved crawling in and out of loco engines all day, was the most dedicated sportsman I have ever met, often leaving home at four in the morning to run to work, then running home again at night and totting up huge weekly training mileages. Each Saturday he met brother Joe for a training run, when they would compare notes for the week, Joe having run perhaps 120 miles and Arthur a few more. One week when he was on holiday Joe experimented with even more miles than usual so when they met and Arthur reported he had run 138 miles, Joe replied that he had clocked up 168.

'Ridiculous,' said Arthur, 'nobody needs to do that many miles,' and he continued to chunter throughout the rest of the run, but the following Saturday he had his revenge when the usual comparison took place.

'Back to normal this week, about 118,' said Joe, 'how about you?'

'181,' said Arthur, who had not been on holiday. Crazy perhaps, but that was what made him a world-class runner and an incredibly tough competitor. As I write, Arthur, nearer ninety than eighty, still keeps fit and a chat with him would inspire any aspiring distance runner. Dominic, the youngest of the Keily boys, was my closest friend and we trained together most days of the week. Dom was destined for great things, winning Great Britain vests and being deprived of chances at Olympic level only by a chronic back injury. A few years older than me, Dominic was one of the last to be called up for national service, but he was soon excused boots, then uniform and so far as I could see duties as well because he seemed to spend most of his time at home training. Shortly before the inter-services championships at Aldershot, Dom convinced me I should travel down with him and stay with the Army team at the barracks, 'where nobody will know who you are anyway'. I was nineteen at the time, possibly twenty, and the implications of this did not enter my head until I found myself in a queue for bedding at Malta Barracks. 'Name?' I was asked when I got to the head of the queue. 'Edwards,' I replied, 'RAOC Chilwell'. My name was ticked off and I disappeared hurriedly, not at all sure I had done the right thing by embarking on this venture. About an hour later a lad called Terry Edwards arrived complaining bitterly that somebody had signed for his gear, 'but somebody's coming over to sort it out,' so I got changed and went out for a long training run. I kept out of sight for a day or two but didn't hear any more and eventually spent the best part of a week there, eating like a king and training twice a day. What the penalty was at the time for impersonating a member of Her Majesty's forces I'm not sure. I preferred not to think about it when I returned to civilian life. The two highlights of the year were the London-to-Brighton and Manchester-to-Blackpool road relays, both of which sadly had to be scrapped in the mid-sixties as the roads became increasingly clogged by traffic. The 'Brighton', which was the AAA championship, was a great spectacle, followed by hundreds of cars and coaches, and Derby were regular winners. One year Mike Bullivant gave the great Bruce Tulloh almost a minute's start and caught him over a six-mile stage. It was the best road relay run I have ever seen and it was no surprise when a few months later Mike broke the world six-mile record in an epic race at the White City. But if the 'Brighton' was the best race, the Manchester-to-Blackpool relay was the most enjoyable. Derby were slowly matched – then overtaken – by Coventry Godiva Harriers and it was tradition for both teams to meet after the race at the Winter Gardens where we succeeded in proving that highly trained runners do not make good drinkers. It was on one of these trips I struck up a lifelong friendship with Coventry's Bill Adcocks, who was to become one of Britain's greatest marathon runners, arguably the greatest. Bill finished fifth in the 1968 Olympic marathon, staged scandalously at altitude in Mexico City. He was the first sea-level-based athlete to finish and it was widely agreed he would have won had it been a fair race. A year later he took on all four who beat him that day when they all lined up in the Athens marathon and though the race was run in very hot and humid conditions he paralysed them, winning by more than two minutes and setting a record which stood for thirty-five years until it was narrowly beaten in the 2004 Olympics. Remarkable. I was never remotely in Bill's class but I can claim that I was only a yard behind him towards the later stages of the inter-counties twenty-mile championship in 1965. There must have been an injury crisis that year, because I was one of the three-man Derbyshire team for the championship which involved running ten two-mile laps of Victoria Park in East London. The race started at six o'clock. It was a hot, sticky evening and, knowing nothing about nutrition, I had decided a light salad would provide the ideal preparation, the exact opposite of carbohydrate packing, which was then unheard of. I was pretty fit and sailed along comfortably for about sixteen or seventeen miles, then practically ground to a halt, dehydrated and totally out of fuel. I struggled on, like Beau Geste staggering through the desert, then heard the pitter patter of flying feet coming up behind and a quick 'come on, George, nearly there' in the broadest Coventry accent as Bill and teammate Juan Taylor cruised past. Not quite, Bill. You were nearly there. I was two miles behind. Having somehow made it to the finish, I stretched out on a bench in the changing rooms for a breather and the next I knew the park-keeper was shaking me by the shoulder, trying to wake me because he wanted to lock up. It was almost dark and, apart from us, the place was deserted. Everybody had gone to the post-race reception (including my teammates and the team manager) so I had to struggle out of sweaty kit, put on some civvies and get myself back to the middle of London. This I eventually managed, only after stumbling out of the tube at Lancaster Gate, falling to my knees and being violently sick all over the platform. It was not the memorable British Games debut I had planned.

CHAPTER 3

THE STORER WAY

Wilf Shaw was not a robust man. He suffered from heart trouble and I am not sure his enthusiasm for horses and greyhounds helped. He also had to cope with the formidable Harry Storer, who ran Derby County rather as Sir Alex Ferguson was to run Manchester United. Harry was always 'Mr Storer' to Wilf, who was clearly in awe of this hard and uncompromising figure, who tended to sign equally hard and uncompromising players.

Glyn Davies, with whom even Norman Hunter and Tommy Smith might have thought twice about tangling, was a wing half more ruthless than any I have seen. Now a great pal living in retirement in Swansea, Glyn, who was at the Baseball Ground when Storer arrived, once had eight stitches in a nasty knee injury and ruled himself out for at least two weeks. Storer had other ideas and told Glyn he would be playing the following Saturday and when, on the morning of the match, Glyn explained the wound had not healed and the stitches would come out after just a few minutes, Storer waved away his protests – 'That's all right, we'll get it stitched up again at half-time.' Storer regarded a touch of brutality as a perfectly acceptable form of defending, indeed it was a prerequisite. At one stage he fielded a half-back line which read Upton, Moore and Davies and had there been much in the way of television coverage at that time, Derby County matches could only have been shown after the 9p.m. watershed and even then viewers of a nervous disposition would have been urged to look away. Frank 'The Tank' Upton, tall and powerfully built, was more than merely a hard man, which is why Chelsea paid good money to give him a chance in the First Division, but he was best known for his tackling. Let's just say it was uncompromising. Moore, who came to League football late, was a huge, lumbering man who clattered anybody in his way. Upton, Moore and Glyn Davies – few marks for artistic impression, but innumerable marks and impressions left on the opposition, not that this reputation ever deterred Glyn from looking back fondly on the occasional bloodbath:

> That was how the game was in those days. It was take no prisoners. We once played at Portsmouth and they had a wing half with quite a reputation. Frank Upton went to get him, but came off worst and was carried off with a serious injury, so it was my turn next. Me and the Portsmouth lad met head-on and we both went down in agony. Next thing there were two stretchers coming on to the field and we were following Frank to hospital. All three of us needed operations and we all woke up next morning in adjoining beds.

On one occasion Davies found himself ordered to kick an opponent – not by Storer but by the opposition manager. He was due to turn out for the reserves against Manchester United reserves, when about half an hour before the kick-off, reserve-team trainer Jack Bowers told him Jimmy Murphy wanted to see him. Murphy, United's assistant manager, was a pal of Glyn's through the Welsh connection and explained that they had a promising young winger in their side, 'but he's a real big-head who thinks he knows it all. He needs bringing down a peg or two, so go out and kick him round the pitch for ninety minutes.' He should have realised that Glyn was planning to do that in any case. That was the Storer way and it suited Glyn perfectly. I had to ring Storer for team news when Wilf was off work, something I enjoyed doing though it made me a little nervous. Told one day that Jack Parry was fit again after a nasty knock, I wrote, 'Jack Parry has recovered from a leg injury and returns to Derby County's team for tomorrow's match against…' Later that day the telephone rang and it was Harry Storer demanding to talk to me. 'I told you Jack Parry was fit, I didn't tell you he was playing,' he said. 'How long have you been picking the team?' He was quite right and I learned a lesson, though Parry did play, of course.

Summers were less eventful. I covered golf, tennis, rowing – anything and everything, really, and it was also my job on Monday mornings to write the local cricket round-up. This meant getting up earlier than usual and cycling to the Post Office depot close to the railway station to pick up all the mail for the *Telegraph*, which was always handed over without any request for identification. It was in a large, heavy bag, which I hung over one handlebar before wobbling the mile or so down to the office. The next task was to weed out all the cricket reports, select the best performances and write a piece which had to be ready by about ten o'clock. There were several regular contributors and one in particular was an unashamed self-publicist. 'Another brilliant innings by Frank Harwood, which included great shots all round the wicket...' or 'only a disgraceful lbw decision denied stylish Frank Harwood...' and even once 'the absence of the dashing Frank Harwood through injury...'. There was one every week, all of them signed 'yours sincerely, Frank Harwood'. To be fair, he was a good batsman.

Football soon resumed and after a stint reporting Chesterfield I was offered a change. I would now be covering whichever of the Nottingham clubs was at home, which was quite an opportunity because Forest were in the First Division, so at the age of nineteen or twenty I was watching Manchester United, Chelsea and Arsenal for a living and sitting in the press box alongside some of my schoolboy heroes, notably Desmond Hackett of the *Daily Express* who, I quickly noted, talked incessantly throughout every match and hardly saw anything that went on. The arrival of Spurs, then the giants of English football, was a great occasion. There were scores of young autograph hunters waiting as the Spurs coach arrived and I expected the players to rush past them into the ground, but quite the opposite happened. John White, the wonderfully gifted Scot who died tragically young after being struck by lightening on a golf course, lined up the players, and they signed autographs for at least ten minutes. Among them was the great Dave Mackay. Little did I realise that a few years later I would be drinking with him and writing his programme notes.

I had struck up close friendships with two fine sports reporters working for the local news agency, Mike Carey and Barry Eccleston, fully paid-up social animals and top-class drinkers, from whom I learned much, along with Barry Askew, another first-rate journalist with a liking for a pint and a pretty face. It was over a pint in The Bell, the hub of all that happened in Derby, that we decided to form a football team and so Derby Pressmen came into being. We put together a makeshift side with Eccleston, who was an excellent player and very light on his feet for a big man, on the right wing, and Carey, who was neither of these, on the left. I was right half and Askew, who was good enough to play non-League semi-pro football to a high standard, was centre forward. We found seven more from somewhere before taking on Sheffield Press at what was known, in those days before political correctness, as the Deaf and Dumb Ground on Ashbourne Road, more accurately a pitch owned by the Royal School for the Deaf, lost 6-1 and departed afterwards somewhat crestfallen to drown our sorrows. We needed reinforcements and I knew where to find them. By the time we had arranged another game, I had whistled up Peter Ekins, the one-time England Boys final triallist, plus Barrie Roughton and Tony Cleaver, two products of the brilliant Gayton Avenue School football academy, all three of whom were playing for the successful Littleover Old Boys team (later Littleover British Legion). Within a season or so, having acquired a few more good players, we were travelling the country hammering all opposition out of sight and remarkably Peter, Barrie and Tony turned up every Sunday morning despite having played the previous day, often presenting themselves in the Market Place at 9a.m. to travel somewhere like Peterborough or Grimsby. Soon we faced our biggest challenge, an away game against the supposedly unbeatable Manchester Press, who included former Manchester United reserve Freddie Pye, a sprinkling of Cheshire League players and Peter Doherty's son Paul at centre forward. Putting on our kit at Manchester United's famous Carrington training ground, where men like Duncan Edwards, Tommy Taylor and Roger Byrne, all victims of the Munich air disaster, had changed for training and where Bobby Charlton still did, was a curious sensation, but perhaps it inspired us because we became the first team ever to beat them. Shortly afterwards Pye, then player-manager of Stalybridge Celtic in the Cheshire League, signed Barrie Roughton, who became a regular for them, yet Barrie – 'Radge' Roughton to all – continued to turn out for us each Sunday

Ever ambitious, Derby Pressmen arranged a charity match against a Show Business team that included Tommy Steele, then keenly promoting his musical *Half a Sixpence*. Several of us had an attack of nerves when we arrived at the ground to discover a crowd of two or three thousand, but we were much better than them even though they had a couple of ex-pros for ballast, and were leading 4-1 halfway through the second half. This was not going according to the script and referee Tim Ward, who had succeeded Harry Storer as Derby County manager, realised this and gave three penalties against us, enabling Tommy Steele to score a hat-trick. My abiding memory of the game was putting my foot on the ball and falling over it. Temporarily embarrassed, I flicked my heel out and caught a young character actor called Harry Fowler a fierce blow on the ankle which earned me a volley of cockney abuse and a stern look from Tim Ward. Fowler was a star of the popular TV comedy *The Army Game* and I noticed he was still limping heavily when it was shown two or three weeks later. We laid on quite a lavish buffet after the game, but all the show business players bar one had gone in no time. The one who stayed and enjoyed himself was the only real star among them, Tommy Steele, who chatted happily to everybody.

Shortly before this we had moved to Matlock, where my father worked. This was where Barry Askew lived and on the way back from one match Barry asked how I fancied a stint freelancing, because Matlock appeared to be virgin territory. As I was earning next to nothing I agreed immediately and though the experiment lasted little more than a year it was worth it for one thing if nothing else – a genuine world scoop. We had good contacts in the Bakewell area and one day it was let slip to us that something odd was going on at Edensor, a tiny village built in the shadow of Chatsworth House, home of the Duke of Devonshire. The villagers had been asked to build a footbridge across a stream which separated the village from a flat piece of land close by. Why? There was a clue. President Kennedy was visiting Britain and we knew his sister Kathleen was buried in the Edensor churchyard. She had married into the family, but died very young in a plane crash. A little snooping and all became clear. JFK was in Manchester on the Saturday morning and due in London later in the afternoon so an unscheduled stop at Chatsworth was planned. We turned up, photographer Ken Upton in tow, a helicopter landed and out stepped the President to a smattering of applause from a few villagers. He wandered past, stopping and shaking hands with a few, and answered our innocuous questions. His shirt collar, I noticed, was at least one size too big and he was not as tall as I expected. After a few minutes he moved away, laid some flowers on his sister's grave, returned to the helicopter and was gone. Within five months he was dead, terribly vulnerable even in relatively security-conscious America. In those innocent, trusting days there were no security checks at Chatsworth and in the occasional perverse moment, it has struck me that any one of us could have shot him. The story and pictures went everywhere because nobody else got wind of this and suddenly lots of money poured in, which enabled me to buy my first car. This was rather putting the cart before the horse because I couldn't drive, but I learned fairly soon. It was a shock when Barry Askew suddenly announced he was moving on. He had been offered a top job on the *Sheffield Telegraph* and was proposing to take it. As a twenty-one-year-old left high and dry this knocked me sideways, but I soldiered on, earning a decent living, until out of the blue I was contacted by my old boss at the *Evening Telegraph* who wondered whether I was interested in rejoining the sports desk. It was one of the easier decisions I have had to make and as I was appointed deputy sports editor shortly afterwards, things seemed to be looking up. As for Barry, he was a very bright man, seemingly destined for great things and over the next few years he achieved a huge amount. He left Sheffield to edit the *Lancashire Evening Post* where he won several awards and was then appointed editor of the *News of the World* so seemed to have everything he could ever have wanted, but Barry had always found it difficult to walk past an open pub and there were plenty of those in Fleet Street. He struck up an odd relationship with Sonia Sutcliffe, wife of Peter Sutcliffe, the Yorkshire Ripper, and took all too easily to the liquid lunches for which the newspaper industry is notorious. He featured regularly in *Private Eye*, was politically at odds with the right-wing views of Rupert Murdoch, and before long was back in Lancashire looking for a job. Like many who have done tolerably well in the regional press, I occasionally flirted with the idea of working in London, in fact I turned down the chance to join the *Sun*, following an offer from sports editor Frank Nicklin, a former *Derby Telegraph* sports writer, which came totally out of the blue. Barry Askew's miserable joust with Fleet Street confirmed my belief that it was not for me.

CHAPTER 4

CORINTHIAN DAYS... THE KING ARRIVES

Back in Derby I settled into the old routine, sub-editing, covering several sports and reporting Derby County Reserves on a Saturday. Much was made of reserve-team coverage in those days and, of course, it meant close and regular contact with the club and the players, which suited me fine, as did the opportunity to get regular treatment for the running injuries I kept picking up. The job was nothing like as stressful or time-consuming as it is for regional journalists these days. More often than not we started work at 9a.m., had an hour or so for lunch and knocked off about 5.30p.m. Wilf Shaw's health had by now deteriorated to such an extent that he had been moved from the sports department to a desk job with the general news subs and Bob Farmer, a youngster from Sussex had taken over. Bob was a pleasant lad who played left-back in our Pressmen football team, always appearing with shorts rolled up as far as possible and hair immaculate. His secret – those days such things were kept secret – was revealed when during one post-match drinks session he was spotted by a prominent member of the local gay scene and that was that. It made no difference to us, but sadly and quite unnecessarily he found it hard to cope and returned to his former paper in Sussex as soon as the opportunity arose before moving on to the *Daily Mirror*. Sadly he died from an Aids-related disease when still only in his early fifties. Bob's decision to leave Derby did, however, leave me realising that with a bit of luck I was going to get the job I always wanted and so it turned out. There was no announcement or song and dance about it. I just stepped up from the reserves to the first team rather as a player might, so just seven years after leaving school I had the job I had dreamed about as a ten-year-old.

Reporting Derby County matches provided an enjoyable if fairly predictable way of earning a living in the early and mid-sixties. Tim Ward, who had enjoyed a highly successful career as a player at the Baseball Ground, managed much as he played, for while he was determined and stylish, hard-working and eternally optimistic, he was essentially a man of old-fashioned values who would have been most at home with the Corinthian Casuals. If somebody had decreed that football was to follow the example of rugby union and each team should clap the other from the pitch at the end of a match, nobody would have been happier than Tim. For him the game was everything and it was he who set up the Derby County Former Players' Association, with which he remained heavily involved until his death. He disliked confrontation, which in some walks of life might be a virtue, but made managing footballers and handling directors difficult if not impossible. He seemed to run the team rather as if it was a 1950s boys' club and was only really happy with players unlikely to rock the boat. But if Ward could get away with trying to create a team of Stepford Husbands, he was much less at ease coping with an archetypal board of directors, businessmen with egos but little or no knowledge of the game. Inevitably his successes worked against him. As the directors saw it, if he could sign outstanding players like Alan Durban and Eddie Thomas for next to nothing, why could he not scout around for more? Why spend big money when he could pick up a top-notch local youngster like Peter Daniel or a non-League goalkeeper as talented as Colin Boulton? Not that Tim scouted round for Boulton, whose signing came courtesy of a recommendation by Nigel Cleevely, a young left-winger he picked up from Cheltenham. Nigel played only a handful of games for the Rams, but he did the club a great favour by telling Tim he had a pal back in Gloucestershire who was a good goalkeeper. And good he certainly was. 'Bernie' (as in Bernie the Bolt from TV show *The Golden Shot*) had to be patient while Les Green was keeping goal superbly, but when his chance came he took it both hands in every sense and was the only player to appear in all 84 matches of Derby's two First Division Championship-winning seasons.

Ward could scarcely dream of the First Division, let alone the title. He struggled on, keeping the club in the Second Division – today's Championship – with a squad of players drawn largely from within a few miles of the Baseball Ground, with Geoff Barrowcliffe, Jack Parry, Ray Young, Ronnie Webster, Mick Hopkinson, John Richardson, Phil Waller, Ian Buxton and Daniel leading the way. They were all extremely good players (Barrowcliffe, Parry and Webster each made more than 500 first-team appearances) and it remains a mystery why the supply of local talent should eventually dry up almost completely, the only consolation being it appears to have dried up everywhere else as well. They were an interesting mix. On away trips, usually made by coach, the front seat was always occupied by Reg Matthews, who sat there so he could be first off, already reaching for his cigarettes. Reg was one of Britain's great goalkeepers in the 1950s and remarkably won the first of his England caps when playing for Coventry City in the Third Division. He signed for Chelsea for £20,000 – then a record for a goalkeeper – and later moved to Derby where he did a wonderful job. When Reg came for the ball he did it in style and anybody who got in his way – teammate or opponent – had to suffer the consequences. Centre half Ray Young said it was like being hit by a bag of scrap metal, while on one occasion, after being clobbered by Reg in an away match at Plymouth, Ronnie Webster was rendered incapable of offering any sort of description as he could hardly speak. Reg came out to punch a cross away and caught Webster smack on the side of the head and though Ron played on after lengthy treatment, he was far from alright. That night we all went to the cinema while waiting for the sleeper back to Derby and I offered one of my sweets to Ron, who was sitting next to me. He muttered his thanks, but didn't utter another word throughout the film. It turned out that his jaw was fractured.

So while Reg sat on the team coach by himself, where he couldn't do any damage, some players joined the manager for a few hands of bridge, something of a rarity in the football world then and even more so now one imagines, while others played brag, a few read and Jack Parry sat on his own and stared out of the window all the way to and from places as far away as Portsmouth and Norwich, even when it was pitch dark, never speaking to a soul. Parry, from a famous Derby football family, was a remarkable man, who played 517 games for the club, a record at the time he retired and a figure that would have been even greater had he not spent a long time out of the game with a serious back injury. He was not a social animal away from football, had something of a 1940s dress sense and never learned to drive, but had a very sharp wit. On the way to one game Eric Kitchen, the club's regular driver, had to swerve sharply to avoid a cyclist and careered into a post box sending letters flying all over the pavement. 'See if there's anything for me, Eric,' shouted Parry almost before the bus had come to a halt.

Those away trips were enjoyable for all sorts of reasons. Not only did I have a chance to mix with the players and have a look round places I had never been to before, I had never stayed in a proper hotel in my life until taking this job and Tim had a fondness for nice hotels and good restaurants, so much so that when a promotion or relegation issue was settled his first reaction might be disappointment that the following season he would be deprived of dinner at the George at Stamford or a night at the Randolph in Oxford. While the game was obviously professional, it had something of an amateurish feel in those days. Many clubs had part-time players, in Derby's case Ian Buxton, the Derbyshire cricket captain, one of the last to combine cricket and football professionally, and John Bowers, who was an advertising salesman on the *Evening Telegraph*. Players turned up for home games in dribs and drabs, having been left to their own devices in the morning. One Saturday morning about 11.30 I popped out of the office to buy a sandwich and bumped into Bobby Ferguson laden down with shopping. Bob introduced me to his wife, chatted briefly, then made his apologies because he had to dash home. Indeed he had, because he was playing left-back that afternoon and the kick-off was about three hours away.

Few clubs had assistant managers back then. Tim's backroom team consisted of trainer Ralph Hann (father of the successful TV presenter Judith, who made her name fronting *Tomorrow's World*), assistant trainer Jack Bowers, who had been one of the game's great pre-war centre forwards, and chief scout Sammy Crooks. Sammy, who would have been a serious contender in any world's nicest man competition, had been a brilliant right-winger and was unlucky to win only 26 England caps. As a scout he was far from a workaholic, but he was a charming man who knew the game inside out and, like so many great players, could never quite grasp why lesser talents could not master what he saw as natural, basic skills. I was once at Derby's Sinfin Lane training ground, where Sammy, well into his sixties, was supervising a session for youngsters and becoming increasingly frustrated that not one seemed able to cross the ball accurately. Eventually he called the boys together and told one of them to stand on the penalty spot and not move. He then placed two balls near the corner flag, signalled to the lad to get ready and with his right foot centered the first straight into his arms. He then repeated the performance with his left foot, all this in a suit and a pair of battered old suede shoes. 'There you are, it's as easy as that,' he said. Easy for him perhaps. When I reminded Sam of this a couple of years later he admitted that it was not just luck or natural talent that enabled him to pull off this particular party trick. As a kid, part of his training routine had been to spend hours trying to cross a ball into an empty barrel that had been placed in the penalty area. Maybe some present-day players should give it a try. Tim, Sammy, Ralph and Jack were all delightful men, but there was not an aggressive streak nor even a spark of devil between the four of them, so not surprisingly Derby County drifted along, winning a few, drawing a few and losing rather too many. Nobody was surprised and fans largely accepted it, because Derby had for some time been an average team apparently destined to remain average. But there was a pleasant surprise round the corner, one which in some respects marked the beginning of a new and hugely exciting Derby County.

For some months Ward had been trying to persuade his directors to sign a young striker from a lower division, but chairman Sam Longson and his colleagues were horrified at the prospect of paying as much as £40,000 for one player. Perhaps normally Ward would have shrugged his shoulders and looked elsewhere, but this time he dug his heels in a little more firmly than usual and eventually got his way, so on a sunny September day in 1966, Kevin Hector, then just twenty-one, left Bradford to become a Derby County player. In those days most transfers were simply announced by way of a call to the local newspaper, but not this time for this was a record signing and Hector was to be unveiled at the Clarendon Hotel. Local freelance Neil Hallam and I duly appeared, were handed a sherry at the door and immediately ushered into a room where he stood eyeing the buffet, thinking how unusual it was for the club to organise anything so lavish and wondering where the others were. A few minutes later a few strangers strolled in and we spotted behind them a man in morning suit and a young lady in a wedding dress. Right hotel, wrong room, and after finishing the sherry we slipped away. Hector made his debut away at Crystal Palace on 17 September. Derby were largely outplayed and he saw little of the ball, but his few touches and sharp pace suggested that Ward had signed a very good player. Seven days later this was to be confirmed in a more spectacular way then anybody could have imagined. Kevin Hector's home debut against Huddersfield Town will long be remembered by all who were there, players, spectators and probably match officials, too. It was like something from Roy of the Rovers as Hector simply tore Huddersfield apart with an astonishing virtuoso display. In footballing terms he appeared to be from another planet, his speed, skill, vision and shooting power unlike anything seen at the Baseball Ground since the days of Raich Carter and Peter Doherty. Derby won 4-3 and poor Alan Durban scored a brilliant hat-trick which was simply lost in the thrill of the occasion. As the final whistle went and Hector jogged towards the tunnel after a truly monumental perform-ance, the crowd stood and roared approval, hardly believing what they had seen. It was quite a day and I was able make the easiest of predictions in my match report: 'Derby County at last have a true star. This is the sort of player who will make sports fans leave comfortable chairs and warm firesides in the winter to stand in the cold on the terraces.' The fans agreed and in an instant coronation Kevin became 'The King'. He was still The King 581 games and 201 goals later. An hour or so after that first match, interviews over and the crowd dispersed, I set off to catch the bus back into town. Local journalists in those days did not run cars and neither, evidently, did brilliant young footballers, because there at the bus stop stood Kevin Hector, waiting for a bus to the railway station. No hotel for the night, not even a lift to the station for the new hero, just a bus ride which he paid for himself. What would today's players make of that? Kevin did not say a lot during that bus ride, but then he never did say a lot. Throughout his career he remained a fairly shy man and it was never easy to judge how much he enjoyed celebrity. He married young, soon after moving to Derby, and it seemed that for the most part his family was all he needed.

While Kevin was making his way back to Bradford, the Baseball Ground boardroom was awash with happy directors and Ward felt vin-dicated, as well he might. He had made several shrewd signings before, one or two very successful, but there had been nothing remotely like this. The following Monday Tim and I met at the Kardomah for cof-fee as usual and he was as excited yet relaxed as I had ever seen him. 'Perhaps this is really the start of a genuine change at this club,' he said and how right he was, but not in the way he hoped. Kevin Hector was to become Tim Ward's ball and chain. A decent crowd of 15,029 had watched Hector's home debut. The next home game brought in 18,442, the one after that 22,949. The directors rubbed their hands. Their investment was paying quick dividends. But though the crowds poured in and results improved a little, the genuine change that Ward had hoped for did not materialise. It was not long before chairman Longson and some of his colleagues were claiming credit for the transfer, Longson once insisting to me that it was entirely down to him and that he had to convince the manager that Hector was worth signing. That was a bit rich to put it mildly, because Ward had told me privately weeks before how frustrated he was over the board's lack of interest in a brilliant young striker he was trying to sign. No doubt all this got back to Ward and assuming it did then even a man of his equable temperament must have felt exasperated, but what he could not dispute was that a final position of seventeenth was very disappointing and worse still he was out of contract. It was to be a summer of change. Ward's contract was not renewed and he left chuntering loudly about not even being able to buy a first-class postage stamp without approval at a full board meeting. 'And yet they seem to think I can go to any little club and buy another Kevin Hector,' he added, a rare show of bitterness by an undemonstrative man. The reality was that Tim Ward, though a good judge of a player and a genuine football person, was unable or unwilling to build a team with a real balance of qualities. He shied away from firebrands, even from real hard men (his old pal Frank Upton apart) and ultimately, while nice guys do not always finish last, they sometimes finish seventeenth.

So who was the new manager to be? The board would not fail to find one for lack of regular meetings for they met every Thursday without fail. This was a routine not followed by all clubs, as illustrated by one splendid occasion when Derby director Sydney Bradley asked the legendary Ipswich Town chairman John Cobbold, master of all he surveyed and much more, how often his board met. 'Twice a year dear boy,' replied Cobbold, who made Noel Coward sound like Jade Goody, 'once in October to draw up the Christmas present list and once in April to decide whether we need a new mower,' a response littered with frequent expletives, high pitched chortles and swigs from his never empty glass of champagne. Bradley, stunned by this revelation, withdrew sharply, but he could claim before too long that he, Longson and their colleagues had their moments of inspiration, too. One Saturday evening a few weeks after Ward's departure I was at home in Matlock when the telephone rang. It was Len Shackleton, once of Sunderland, Clown Prince of

Football and a hero throughout the game, who by then was writing for a Sunday newspaper. 'I thought you might like to know who your new manager is going to be,' said Shack. 'The bad news is you'll read it in my column tomorrow, the good news is it's Brian Clough.' I was unsure how to respond since I knew nothing about Clough other than that he had been a superb player. I asked what he was like. 'Well,' said Shack, after pausing for a second, 'let's just say he's different.'

CHAPTER 5

FAMILY LINKS, MAD HARRY AND AN EXPENSES PROBLEM

That Derby was always a football town has not been disputed since Steve Bloomer was dazzling crowds more than 100 years ago. When Bloomer joined Derby County the role of manager had not been invented, so the players were looked after on a day-to-day basis by the club trainer, a role enjoyed for a time by my great grandfather Joe, presumably on the basis of his prowess as a professional sprinter, though he evidently followed soccer closely and knew something about the game because records show he recommended some of the players Derby signed. Joe, who later moved to London to train Arsenal, must have been a versatile fellow because he managed to juggle his football commitments with running The Grapes in Green Lane, where he was landlord. Joe's mother died young and his father, also Joe, subsequently married into the Robshaw family, who had come down from Yorkshire in the 1850s and immediately started making money out of scrap. Joe senior's new wife went to her grave illiterate, never having learned even to sign her name, but she had a shrewd business brain and so had her sons, who went on to achieve enormous wealth. Her grandson Ben eventually became chairman of Derby County and was in the thick of the financial scandal that got the Rams into trouble immediately after the Second World War. Ben was banned from football for life, the *Evening Telegraph* reporting at the time that 'he attended a board meeting at the Baseball Ground at which he resigned then returned to his scrap yard in his white Rolls-Royce.' Sadly the Rolls-Royce seems no longer to be in the family. There were other Edwards links to the club. Harry Payne, my father's cousin and a fine footballer with Derbyshire Amateurs, became a Rams director and another cousin, Alex Miller, was for many years assistant secretary at the Baseball Ground, where he and his boss Cyril Annable, with the help of a typist, ran the club between them without any obvious alarms. These days, for some reason, it seems to require a small army to keep a football club ticking over.

The club, very much like the town itself, was comfortable, set in its ways, unchanging and nondescript. The Swinging Sixties they may have been, but while Liverpool was reinventing popular music and Carnaby Street turning fashion upside down, Derby plodded unspectacularly on, Rolls-Royce and the railway industry ensuring as near to full employment as made no difference, indeed it was widely accepted that anybody could get a job at Rolls-Royce simply by turning up. Social life meant going either to one of Derby's numerous cinemas, or a jazz club – 'trad' was very much the rage – or dressing up a bit and choosing between the Locarno, which was a quite modern dance hall in Babington Lane, and the ramshackle Trocadero on Normanton Road. The Troc, as it was inevitably known, was run by the equally ramshackle Sammy Ramsden, who had moved to Derby from Bolton back in the 1920s as a door-to-door tonic wine sales-man having made and lost money all over the country. He opened the Plaza, in London Road, where he managed to get Louis Armstrong to appear, then embarked on all sorts of ventures in the 1950s and '60s, not least finding himself an attractive young wife. Sam surprised everybody, himself included, some suspected, by becoming a father when he was seventy-two, but not even this impressive evidence of youthful energy and a series of public meetings could persuade Derby County to accept him as a director, though he was a genuine supporter and offered to put in £60,000 to buy new players. Sam was a warm character who talked to anybody and everybody. When I once spotted him outside Preston North's Ground on a freezing cold day he suggested a quick snifter to warm us up and while I was looking round to see if there was a pub nearby, opened his voluminous overcoat to reveal bottles of Scotch, Brandy and Rum sticking out of inside pockets along with a couple of beakers.

Generally, however, there was little money about. Thousands of houses still did not have bathrooms and Derby, like so many towns and cities at the time, was also grappling with the effects of immigration, which had brought black and Asian faces to the scene on an unprecedented scale. In the early part of the 1960s, the area around the Baseball Ground was still predominantly white, but that was to change and not everybody liked it. In my possibly naïve way I put this down to fear of the unknown and still believe I was right. It was not strictly racism, just out-and-out colour prejudice and, of course, completely ignored the fact that Derby was just one of numerous industrial towns which had sought overseas workers after the war because of a shortage of manpower and that those workers had always been given the poorly paid so-called 'dirty' jobs. Social historians have rewritten the 1960s, conveniently forgetting the huge scale of homelessness which led to so many children being taken into care, the poor housing, the low levels of pay and almost constant industrial unrest, but it was a memorable decade for all that. The Great Train Robbery and the Profumo scandal both excited and appalled us, while we mourned the death of Churchill, wept for the children of Aberfan, were stunned by the assassination of Kennedy and thrilled when America put a man on the moon. Those of us for whom sport mattered perhaps more than it should marvelled at the skills of Arnold Palmer, a young Jack Nicklaus, George Best, Jimmy Greaves, Garry Sobers and Cassius Clay and celebrated wildly when Geoff Hurst's hat-trick won the World Cup for England at Wembley. In steadfastly parochial Derby we also mourned in our own way the closure of Friargate railway station under the Beeching proposals. There was even a plan to demolish the magnificent Friargate bridge, but public outcry and a well-organised campaign ensured its survival. An era ended, too, with the disappearance from the streets of the wonderful trolley buses, which caused havoc to traffic whenever one of the poles became detached from the wires and total chaos if there was a power cut, but were nothing if not environmentally friendly. And I was certainly not the only person to be saddened by the decision to demolish Cockpit Hill so that the Eagle Centre could be built.

For those of a certain age, Cockpit Hill simply was Derby. There, at the Saturday-morning market, Mad Harry had for years held centre stage, selling household goods – usually crockery – at knock-down prices, his mesmeric style attracting flocks of shoppers. 'Not ten shillings, not seven and six, not even five bob. This teapot will cost you not four bob, not three bob. I'll tell you what I'll do. Two and six. Just two and six. Half-a-dollar. And I've only got two, now's your chance,' and so it went on, Harry frequently hurling plates to the floor as he spoke, smashing them to smithereens, all part of the showmanship of a classic market trader. Inevitably as shoppers moved on and others replaced them he found a couple more of these supposedly scarce teapots and continued to do so at regular intervals throughout the day. He probably sold them all, because people seemed to fall over themselves to hand over their money. As a lad in my early teens I could watch him for ever. On Sunday afternoons we would sit in Cockpit Hill's seedy café sipping milkshakes and putting the occasional shilling in the jukebox while watching out for Pigeon Percy, a sad old figure, tall but stooping under the weight of his scruffy overcoat and always throwing seed down for the pigeons. Nobody seemed to know who Percy was or where he lived, though we all greeted him cheerfully and he always grunted a civil response. When Cockpit Hill disappeared, he disappeared with it and I don't remember ever seeing him again. I suspect his name wasn't Percy at all, it just fitted in its alliterative way with pigeon so that was what everybody called him.

Cockpit Hill at night was quite a different place, though I was certainly not aware of that as a schoolboy. The Canal Tavern, which I later found to be considerably seedier than the café, attracted some decidedly unsavoury characters, including women who frequented it in order to further their career prospects. As a trainee running copy from the morning session of a trial at the Assize Court, I watched some slow-witted, inarticulate labourer, accused of raping a woman he had met in the Canal Tavern, apparently heading for certain conviction and a gaol sentence. His youthful defence counsel was struggling badly to get any sense out of him at all, but when we all returned after the lunch recess it was soon clear this keen young lawyer had used the break well. He had gone to the Canal Tavern and done some investigating. He immediately recalled the woman who had brought the charges and began by asking something along the lines of 'Do you sometimes find that on a good night you leave the Canal Tavern with more money than you had when you arrived?' which caused some amusement on the press benches. She had been rumbled. Obviously her profession in itself did not necessarily mean the charge was false, but the defence was now well on top and the woman's story slowly changed until she eventually agreed that everything that had happened had been more or less mutually agreed. Earlier there had been another mildly comic moment when the woman explained that the supposed attack had taken place when she was pushed against a wall. The judge looked surprised by this and intervened to ask, 'are you telling us that this entire encounter took place standing up? You were vertical throughout?' It was a long time ago but one remembers that sort of thing. The accused man watched the entire cross-examination in a strangely detached way, rather as if it all concerned somebody else. He was duly acquitted and left the dock looking totally baffled by the entire business, perhaps understandably as he been roaring drunk on the night in question and said he remembered nothing.

So that was Cockpit Hill. Perhaps, on reflection, it was as well it went after all. It was a time when the face of Derby was finally changing and certainly nobody was sorry when the slaughterhouse near Bass's Rec was finally closed. The Derby Hum was infamous and the slaughterhouse was the cause. Bones were burned there and when the weather was warm and the wind in the wrong direction the smell was absolutely revolting. I can smell it now, sickly and enough to turn the strongest stomach. People said, and with every good reason, that the smell from British Celanese was horrible, but it was nothing compared with the Derby Hum, which would clear the nearby pubs in minutes if it suddenly came on strong. We at the *Telegraph* had no escape from this dreadful smell while we were at work, our only option being to keep the windows closed. In those days the offices were still in Albert Street, where the elderly presses turned out almost 100,000 copies a day, a figure unimaginable today. The paper had few pages back then, often only sixteen on a Monday and rarely more than twenty-eight or thirty-two at the end of the week, but it seemed everybody bought it. It was an extraordinary mish-mash, with the sport split up, some on page two (opposite women's topics), perhaps a bit more somewhere in the middle of the paper and the rest inside the back page opposite the births, marriages and deaths. The wife of the Bishop of Derby was for some reason commissioned to write a column, the Junior Telegraph Club took up a whole page with its painting competition and letter from Auntie Doris and Uncle Eric ('Beryl has sent us a jolly postcard in very neat writing to tell us what a lovely time she and her mummy and daddy are having at Mablethorpe'), while more space was devoted to greyhound results from Derby, Somercotes and Long Eaton than to television and radio programmes combined. It all seems rather amateurish now, but it was right for its time as was proved by the remarkable sales figures, which would be the envy of almost any regional newspaper in the country these days. Back then there was little competition from television and no such thing as local radio, in addition to which editors were happy to provide readers with what they wanted – good old-fashioned local news. A perfect example of that came when the *Telegraph* decided to publish each Friday local amateur football team selections for the following day's games. This was a simple but brilliant idea and a sure-fire seller, because players bought the paper not only to find out whether they had been picked, but also to check who was turning out for the opposition. Just eleven names then, of course, followed by the inevitable instruction for those playing away 'Meet Ice Factory 12.15'. There must have been scores of young men milling around the Ice Factory (now the Cockpit Car Park) around midday every Saturday.

Reporters continued to go everywhere by bus since none could afford a car. This meant expense claims had to have bus tickets attached to them by way of verification, but even these meagre payments were handed over grudgingly. In my early days I was sent to the railway station to collect a parcel which, I was told, was needed urgently, so I thought it sensible to catch a bus. When I submitted an expense claim for 4*d* the following week the deputy news editor Les Stiles was most unhappy. Apparently I should have walked the mile or so to the station and back and when I protested that the parcel was needed urgently I was told that I was supposed to be a fit young lad so I should have run. Les Stiles was so unpopular that the trainees once nailed a kipper to the underside of his desk, but he mellowed as he got older and for years it was Les who would take down my Derby County reports when I dictated them from around the country on a Saturday afternoon. He wasn't much good on the news desk, but at least he was a decent typist. The paper's first edition did not come out until just before midday, but production, though technically crude by today's standards, was extremely slick. That Midday edition was quickly followed by the Burton Edition, then the Final, the Burton Final, the Late Final and finally the Extra Special, which printed at 4.40p.m., often containing reports of court hearings that had taken place that afternoon. Six editions a day back then, plus the Football Special on Saturday night – two editions of that, too – which was on the streets by 5.05p.m. How times change.

Things had moved on just a little by the time Brian Clough arrived in the summer of 1967. His appointment did not make front-page news, but there was a streamer heading on the back – 'Brian Clough to be new Rams chief: Peter Taylor his No.2' – which caused the sale of that day's paper to go up by a couple of hundred. From what I recall the news created moderate interest, because there was novelty in having a manager who was only twenty-nine years old, but there was no great excitement. Rams fans, for whom disappointment arrived each year with all the depressing predictability of their tax demand, preferred to wait and see.

CHAPTER 6

HELLO BRIAN... AWAY WE GO

What would I make of Brian Clough and, equally important, what would he make of me? I soon found out, because he telephoned out of the blue one May afternoon. It was a fairly brief conversation.

'George Edwards?'

'Yes.'

'Brian Clough.'

Quite what I said I can't remember. I suppose I had always thought I would have to ring him first, but he had taken the initiative and for the first time I was treated to that curious nasal drawl on the other end of the telephone.

'You don't get on with the chairman?'

'Er… not very well, no,' I admitted.

'Well you shouldn't either,' he said, the first of many times he said something I didn't expect. 'Anyway I'll see you tomorrow. Twelve o'clock down here.'

This was clearly more of an instruction than a request and had I been facing urgent open-heart surgery the following day then apparently I would have to postpone it so far as he was concerned, but the important thing was that contact had been made. Evidently he made a similar call to Neil Hallam, who reported Derby County for Raymonds News Agency and Neil and I went up to the ground together. Twelve o'clock came and went, so did 12.30 and it was almost one before Clough came marching out on to the pitch where we were waiting, with Peter Taylor ambling along just behind. He had the good grace to apologise and I was stupidly tempted to say it didn't matter because we had also been delayed and only just arrived, but good sense prevailed and we just smiled and introduced ourselves. Brian was surprisingly frank. 'I need you two,' he said. 'I'm not interested in national newspapers.' This, in fact, was just as well, because they were not interested in him either. He had done a sound job as manager at Hartlepools, his first club, but his reputation was still that of a great goalscorer – statistically English football's greatest ever in terms of goals per game – and not as a manager. We were suitably impressed as he elaborated. He was not looking for biased match reports or favours, but he did want publicity and he wanted to be able to trust us. Any breaches of confidence and the relationship was dead and buried and so on and so on and so on. Peter Taylor stood gazing round the ground, apparently lost in his own world, not listening to a word of this. We then asked a few routine questions to which Cloughie gave equally routine answers and Neil and I headed back to town, not quite sure what to make of it all. At that time little was known outside the north-east of Brian Clough the man and we had not really learned much more. He was twenty-nine and I was twenty-four, Neil Hallam a year or so younger, and the reality was that all three of us were novices in our respective jobs, me especially as I had just taken over as sports editor. There was none of Brian's 'young man' nonsense in those days and neither was there in the years to come in the case of me, Hallam, Carey, Eccleston and my successor Gerald Mortimer. By the time he started using that patronising form of address it was far too late to change his relationship with us. A few days later he called a bigger press conference which possibly attracted as many as half a dozen. By this time he was more relaxed and slightly more confident. He was making no promises but already fed up with people telling him about Derby's great past 'which they only talk about because they have nothing else to talk about'. Well, he was right, but only up to a point. In post-war terms Derby's great past involved only two or three seasons and a spectacular partnership between two all-time greats, Raich Carter and Peter Doherty. Spectacular it might have been but is was also brief and Derby's decline after their FA Cup victory in 1946 was swift, indeed far from talking about the club's great days, most supporters were moaning about the immediate past and the failure to build after winning promotion from the Third Division (North) under Storer. Some time later I told him this and he agreed, claiming he was just trying to make the point that constantly looking back on the good times was no way to build a future.

He also went on at great length about his and Taylor's huge admiration for Storer. The biggest influence on Brian's life in football was Alan Brown, his manager at Sunderland for whom he had enormous respect, but long before Brown came into his life he and Taylor had sought out Harry at every opportunity and picked his brains for all they were worth. Certainly much of the early Clough was pure Storer.

While Cloughie was busying himself round the town (as it then was), Peter Taylor kept a much lower profile during that first summer, but it was soon obvious he had made it his job to cultivate the directors. Sam Longson always enjoyed the limelight, but some of his colleagues were a little less happy, especially when it slowly began to dawn on them that Clough was putting them under pressure. Though he had made no promises at that first press conference, he later started talking via the paper about buying players and not just cast-offs but good players and that disconcerted some of the board, because it would mean spending money, something they were not in the habit of doing. Taylor for a while tried to balance this by chatting to the directors about 'taking us time' to get it right, looking for good local youngsters and building on the squad the club currently had and this, of course, they liked. Then out of the blue he played a killer card by asking me to write a piece praising the board for its ambition. I must have looked surprised, but he knew what he was doing. He gave me a series of quotes, praising Longson and his fellow directors for their vision and determination to see Derby get into the First Division, adding how delighted he was that they recognised the need to sign new players. The piece duly appeared and I can only imagine the blood draining from some of those directors' faces when they read it. They were now caught in a pincer movement between Clough's directness and Taylor's marginally more subtle approach. They simply had to deliver. To be fair to Sam Longson he would not have been too worried by this, because not only did he have plenty of money, he genuinely wanted the club to succeed. Add to that a giant ego that revelled in all this publicity and it was no wonder he became ever more the dominant director as his colleagues shied away from the public's ever increasing levels of expectation. Clough, Taylor and indeed Longson were talking a good game as the new season approached and it was evident the supporters had caught the mood. There was a feeling of relaxed optimism and season tickets were going well even though there had been no signings, then a week before the opening game came a typical Clough telephone call.

'Can you get a photographer down here?'

'I imagine so, why?'

'I've got our new centre forward with me. You'd better get here too, really, hadn't you?'

'So who is it, then?'

'John O'Hare.'

'Right.' Pause at my end

'From Sunderland. £20,000. We've robbed them.'

'Right.' A further pause at my end.

'Heard of him?'

'I'm afraid not. Does he get goals?'

'No, not really.'

'Is he big?'

'No. Well, not tall.'

'Quick?'

'No, far from it.'

'Good in the air?'

'No.'

Cloughie was starting to chuckle at my obvious confusion. 'Just get yourself down here,' he said and the phone went down.

John O'Hare, then just nineteen, made his debut the following Saturday. He went on to make 305 first-team appearances and play for Scotland on 13 occasions. As Brian had said, he was not quick and not tall for a centre forward, though he was powerfully built. He was not a great header of the ball, neither was he a prolific goalscorer, but he was a wonderful player who caused us to marvel as he reduced out-standing centre halves like Ron Yeats and Mike England to stumbling, bumbling impotence. Clough had spotted O'Hare as a fifteen-year-old at Sunderland and recognised in him qualities others obviously missed or did not fully appreciate, which is why he became his first transfer target. John scarcely hesitated before agreeing to sign. 'Brian said Derby would pass Sunderland as we went up and they went down,' he said. 'It didn't quite happen like that, but he was not far off because Sunderland went down that season and we went up the next. It was a move I never regretted for a second.' If John O'Hare had been blessed with pace he would have been an all-time great, because his skill, especially with his back to goal, was extraordinary. He was the perfect target man, superb at using his broad frame to shield the ball, and he was as brave as they come, home or away. He took some batterings from frustrated centre halves, but just picked himself up and got on with it. Eventually he followed Clough to Leeds and then Nottingham Forest where, fittingly, he signed off a wonderful career against Hamburg in Real Madrid's Bernabeu Stadium when he helped Forest to the second of their European Cup triumphs. Not a bad way to go out.

John was known universally as Solly and for a long time the suggestion was that this was because teammates compared him with the great Real Madrid player Luis del Sol. John had a more mundane explanation – that it was a family nickname bestowed on him because he had been born on a Monday (Solomon Grundy, born on Monday. Solly). Many years later, at the Derby County Former Players' Association dinner, Alan Durban read out a list of apologies for absence:

> John O'Hare can't be here tonight. You all remember John, our First Division championship centre forward, Scotland's World Cup centre forward, European Cup winner. John can't be with us this evening because he's working nights. I wonder how many of today's players will be working a night shift in thirty years' time.

A rhetorical question, of course, but at least John was there the following year, clutching a pint as usual. Back in 1967 he was a young man, not quite sure what he had let himself in for having left the north-east football hotbed to join a struggling Second Division club, though he must have been encouraged – as must Longson and his colleagues – when 19,412 turned out to watch the opening game of the season against Charlton Athletic which Derby won 3-2. The fans were encouraged, too, and 21,516 turned up for the following home game. A second signing followed two weeks later, this one a far more unorthodox affair which once more caught me out completely. Again the telephone rang, this time at my home about six o'clock on a Saturday morning, as I was starting to move around, preparing to join the team coach for a trip to Crystal Palace. And again we had one of those odd staccato conversations.

'George. Brian. Bit of news for you.'

'Right…'

'You won't believe this, we've signed Roy McFarland.'

It was John O'Hare all over again. Another stunned silence at my end, then a quick but probably unconvincing recovery.

'Brilliant. How much?'

'Just under £25,000. I thought you might want to get it in today's paper. I'll tell you all about it later. See you in a bit.'

I waited a while then rang the office. 'We've just signed somebody called Roy McFarland,' I said. 'I've never heard of him. I don't know who he plays for, what position he plays, how old he is or anything, but he cost about £25,000. I'm off to London so somebody else will have to write it.'

I didn't get much out of Brian on the way to Crystal Palace because, not surprisingly, he slept for most of the journey, but on the way back he told me all about it. During their time at Hartlepools, Peter Taylor had identified two Fourth Division players he thought capable of playing at a far higher level, Kevin Hector and Roy McFarland. By happy coincidence Hector was already at the Baseball Ground when they arrived, so that just left McFarland, Tranmere Rovers' nineteen-year-old centre half, and there was no time to lose because McFarland was attracting the attention of managers and scouts all over the country. Bill Shankly at Liverpool was one known to be keeping an eye on him, but nobody seemed prepared to take a chance on this raw youngster playing in football's basement division. Not until Clough and Taylor got involved. They travelled to Tranmere that Friday night ostensibly to have a look at McFarland, as many others were doing, but in fact to sign him, not an easy job since the guest seats were packed with football people, so Brian and Peter devised a strategy. In the guestroom after the game they kept an eye on Tranmere manager Dave Russell and when he moved to leave the room Clough followed him while Taylor, ever the entertainer, distracted the other managers by embarking on a rambling anecdote. Clough caught up with Russell in the gents and by the time they returned to the others they were well on the way to striking a deal. Negotiations in Dave Russell's office were fairly brief, ending with Clough putting in a bogus telephone call to Sam Longson (in fact he rang his own home) asking permission to exceed the £20,000 he had been authorised to pay. Agreement was duly reached at £24,500 and Clough was given permission to talk to the player, a conversation the Tranmere manager assumed would take place the next morning. Not likely. Clough and Taylor were not prepared to risk waiting that long and shortly afterwards poor old Russell found himself driving to McFarland's house with Brian and Peter following behind. Still worried that something might go wrong – one or two managers realised something was happening and so did a couple of journalists – Cloughie asked Russell to put would-be pursuers off the scent by initially heading away from the area where McFarland lived and so it was just before one in the morning that they finally turned up outside the home of Les McFarland, a fanatical Everton supporter. Les was roused from his bed by two men he had never seen before in his life and so, a few minutes later, was his tired and rather grumpy son, a keen Liverpool fan whose only ambition was to join Shankly at Anfield. A tough job then, for Clough and Taylor, but they were obviously at their most persuasive and within an hour McFarland had signed, sitting in his pyjamas sipping tea. 'I could have cried in the car on the way back I was so happy,' said Clough. Roy McFarland became a Derby County legend. It is justifiably said that the word 'great' is bandied about far too easily in sport but Roy was by any standards a great player, at least as good on the ball as Rio Ferdinand (far better in the opposition half), lightening quick and as uncompromising as John Terry as a defender while infinitely more skilful. In other words he had everything. He was to make 530 appearances for the Rams and but for injury would have won far more than the 28 England caps that came his way.

There was one more early-season signing of immediate significance. Clough went to Nottingham to sign Alan Hinton, a winger famed for his ferocious shot and the ability to leap out of the way at the slightest hint of a 50/50 tackle. I remember going to Hillsborough to see Hinton, then playing for Wolves, make his debut for England against France at the age of only nineteen. He seemed destined for great things, but lost his way and moved to Forest where he was struggling to rebuild his career when Derby made their approach. There was some celebration, even amusement, in Nottingham when the deal went through and a certain amount of bafflement among Derby supporters. Clough had been almost recklessly fearless in his playing days and had signed two players, O'Hare and McFarland, who never shirked the fiercest challenge, so what was he doing signing a man who seemed to regard physical contact as something to avoid at all costs? This was put to Peter Taylor as diplomatically as possible and his response was a simple one:

If we had wanted a centre forward who was six feet tall and ran like a sprinter we wouldn't have signed John O'Hare. If we had wanted a winger who could tackle we wouldn't have signed Alan Hinton. We signed him because he is a highly talented footballer. Just wait and see.

We did and there was not much doubt as to who was proved right. Hinton could play on either wing because he was equally strong with either foot. David Beckham has often been described as the best crosser of the ball in the world (by England supporters, anyway) and he may indeed have been one of the best right-footed crossers of a dead ball, but Hinton could cross a moving ball, running at speed, from either wing with pinpoint accuracy, often when apparently hemmed in by defenders. It had not always been so. When Alan first joined Wolves his left foot was very much for standing on only, so the coaches made him spend hours practising with his left, even to the extent of sometimes making him wear a boot on his left foot and a plimsoll on his right during training games. It was hard work, but it paid dividends in the end.

Hinton was the great creator, but he was also to score many memorable goals, including one against Everton which was surely one of the best ever seen at the Baseball Ground. Derby attacked down the right through John McGovern, Alan Durban, then Kevin Hector who, seeing his way blocked, cut inside and rolled the ball across to where Hinton was cutting in from the left. Alan was at least thirty-five yards out when he met the ball without breaking stride and hit it with all his considerable power. There was a split-second's silence in the crowd, then an eruption of noise as the ball flew into the top corner and Hinton fell to his knees, seemingly overwhelmed by his own brilliance. Back then, long before the green sweatshirt and dug-out bellowing of his Forest days, Clough would sit impassively in the stand in suit and tie, rarely speaking or moving, but as Hinton knelt motionless, Brian leapt to his feet, arms in the air. It was that sort of moment. More than thirty years later I met a keen Derby County fan I had not seen since leaving school. As we shook hands his first words were 'How are you?' followed very quickly by 'Do you remember that goal Alan Hinton scored against Everton?' Hinton served Derby superbly through all their triumphs and long before he left had established himself as a huge favourite with the supporters, who were more than happy to accept that a lack of enthusiasm for 50/50 tackles was a price worth paying for the goals he scored and created. He departed the Baseball Ground after a testimonial game against an All-Star team watched by 30,000 people and was given a terrific reception as he walked out between a guard of honour. Whoever it was who selected the All-Star team must have had a sense of humour, because lined up at right-back against him was Tommy Smith, Liverpool's unsmiling assassin. Smith, who obviously got the joke, cruised along for about eighty minutes without actually making a tackle, at which point somebody, presumably intentionally, played a ball about twenty yards in front of Alan so he could run on to it. Smith suddenly shot across to intercept and there was an intake of breath around the ground as the prospect loomed of the departing hero leaving the ground for the last time by way of the top tier of the new Ley Stand, but at the last second Smith remembered the script and skidded to a halt. There was much laughter, on the pitch and off, as Alan 'won' the ball and scampered away before putting over another of his wonderful crosses. 'Noddy', as he was known to fans and teammates alike, played 316 first-team games in all. It is quite extraordinary that the first three players signed by Clough and Taylor – O'Hare, McFarland and Hinton – made a total of 1,154 appearances between them. Can any other management team make a claim like that? And so it seemed Derby were set fair for immediate success, because they had real momentum, they were signing good players and the crowds were rolling in. But it was not to be. Clough had made just one pre-season prediction, which was that Derby would finish higher in the Second Division table than they had under Tim Ward the previous year. Well, he got that well and truly wrong.

CHAPTER 7

WE WANT WAGGY

That first season under Clough and Taylor had started deceptively well. There was only one new face, John O'Hare, on the opening day when Derby beat Charlton 3-2, but the quick addition of McFarland had an immediate impact, even though the young centre half had moved up two divisions, and after a 5-1 victory stroll at Cardiff, 28,251 fans turned up to watch the Rams go fourth in the table by beating Rotherham 4-1 at the Baseball Ground. 'The large crowd watched in bored silence,' I wrote at the time, for that was how it was. Derby were not very good, but Rotherham were awful and Taylor in particular was unimpressed. Six wins and a draw from seven games looked fine on paper, but Peter was down in the dumps the following Monday. 'If we keep playing like that we'll get relegated,' he complained. 'We've got three new players [Alan Hinton had made his debut in the Rotherham game], but we need a new team.' This was the typical sweeping generalisation of a football person and less than fair because he and Clough had inherited three superb players in Hector, Durban and Ronnie Webster, plus Reg Matthews, a brave and experienced goalkeeper, and solid Second Division performers like John Richardson, Peter Daniel, Bobby Saxton, Phil Waller and Mick Hopkinson. Wingers Gordon Hughes and Billy Hodgson were certainly past their best by then, but there was still the nucleus of a perfectly good team. Peter's answer – and they were his signings, not Clough's – was to pay Shrewsbury Town £5,000 for Pat Wright and twice that for Arthur Stewart, who had been playing well in Ireland for Glentoran. Wright was superbly fit and good going forward, but struggled defensively while

Stewart was one-pace and as an old-fashioned wing half good enough neither defensively nor in attack. Though he had his moments it was hard to see what Stewart in particular could bring to the side in the long term and the fact that he had a few decent games and won four of his seven international caps while at the Baseball Ground did not change that. The signings smacked of panic and Peter later admitted to breaking one of his cardinal rules in that he had only ever watched Wright in Shrewsbury's home games. Having been signed, they had to play and neither really improved the team very much. Pat Wright, a very personable fellow, later did well in coaching, but managed only 12 League appearances with the Rams. He tried a favourite old pro's trick on the way back from Bolton after only his third appearance, when he sat himself down next to me on the coach at the start of the journey home.

'Well, we're never going to start winning games until we start scoring goals are we, George?' he said in a brisk, businesslike manner, making a particular point of emphasising that he knew my name.

'Well maybe not, no, Pat.'

'It's really hard defending when the forwards don't take pressure off you all game, especially when you're away.'

'I'm sure it is,' I replied, declining to mention something he seemed to have overlooked – that the Rams had scored three goals that afternoon but conceded five and it was his job to try to keep them out. Nice try, Pat, but I was not buying that one. Derby made one other signing at that time. Peter went back to Burton for Richie Barker, who was almost twenty-eight and had spent his entire semi-professional career in non-League football. Richie, a draughtsman by profession, was a highly intelligent, articulate man who was out of the ordinary among footballers if only because he read the *Financial Times* on the team coach. He was also a very good player, a natural goalscorer who would run for ever, home or away, his weakness being that this running was very much of the one-pace variety. He proved a shrewd signing, for his attitude as much as his goals, and when he left the Rams having made a more than useful contribution, went on to earn himself a considerable reputation as a coach, at home and abroad.

After that bright opening to the season Derby started to struggle and it seems I was starting to get as fed up as some of the fans. 'Derby County drifted like eleven sleep-walkers to this defeat showing a complete lack of zest for the game,' I wrote after they were beaten 3-0 at Hull and after the following Saturday's 4-2 home beating by Middlesbrough I tried the heavy sarcasm route in my match report:

> Sir Alf Ramsey and MP George Brown were guests, but it would have made no difference had those two been joined in the directors' box by John Lennon, General de Gaulle and the Black and White Minstrels because no outside influences could have prevented this defeat. And before anybody says the Black and White Minstrels were on the pitch...

All very droll, I must have thought, and a bit patronising, but it did not disturb Clough at all. He didn't say a word. By New Year's Eve (it must have been the confidence of youth), I was almost throwing a challenge down to the new manager because after yet another defeat my report began, 'The truth must be faced. Derby County have some players of greater ability and potential, but the overall product remains much where it was last season under a different regime.' And still there was no reaction from Brian and Peter.

By now young John Robson had come into the side at only seventeen years of age, a risky strategy not really in John's best interests and one which flew in the face of the widely accepted theory that inexperienced youngsters should never be brought into struggling teams. Results and performances remained inconsistent. Early in the new year Cardiff City, who at the start of the season had been beaten 5-1 by Derby at Ninian Park, came to the Baseball Ground and won 4-3. 'The longer the season lasts the more baffling Derby County become,' said my match report. Baffling? I suspect this time I was being overly kind. There were few encouraging signs and with hindsight I wonder how much of this was down to the fact that neither Clough nor Taylor had ever professed to be especially interested in coaching or, come to think of it, even remotely interested in it. Taylor, for all his remarkable football knowledge, only ever offered two words of advice from the touchline, an urgent, staccato shout of 'Owd it' (as in 'hold it'), while Clough lacked the patience to spend hours trying to improve the technical skills of inadequate players. He was always keen for the team to train in the afternoon because matches were usually played in the afternoon, but that was about as sophisticated as it got. What he and Taylor wanted to do – and eventually it was something they achieved with spectacular success at both Derby and Forest – was assemble teams so well balanced and skilful that little or no coaching was required. So while it is obviously true that Clough in particular teased the best out of people, this was more often than not achieved by his motivational methods, sometimes subtle, sometimes crude and, of course, by placing them in the right playing environment. It was the raw material that really mattered. He and Taylor knew, for instance, that Roy McFarland was so good a player that he would improve gradually regardless of what was going on around him, but that he would develop much more quickly when he had more accomplished and experienced people alongside him, as proved precisely the case. But midway through that first season there was no Dave Mackay, no Les Green and precious little to cheer about. The team seemed to lack shape, direction and leadership and what little confidence there was unsurprisingly drained away rapidly as the weeks rolled on. Evidently I was still accepting Clough's invitation to tell it as I saw it. 'If there was any justice at all, some Derby County players would hand over their unopened wage packets to Roy McFarland this week,' was the indignant introduction to my report of a 3-2 home defeat by Ipswich Town. Then a little later, after a truly awful performance at Huddersfield:

> Some of the players seem to think the close season has started already. Many more performances like this and they'll spend that close season preparing for a spell in Division Three. It was left to Roy McFarland to carry the team on his shoulders... a lad of 19.

Fighting talk indeed, but I suppose at least Roy would still have been talking to me. Yet still the crowds turned up. There were plenty of critical letters to the paper and no shortage of tap-room moaners lamenting the lack of progress, not to mention sceptics in the boardroom, but for all the failings there was still a sense among an ever-growing proportion of supporters that success was not too far away. Right to the end of that season disappointment followed disappointment, but not even defeat in each of the final three home games could dampen this spark of optimism. By this time I seemed to have tired of being openly confrontational so all I could manage after Hull had won 2-1 at the Baseball Ground in early April was to begin by declaring that, 'Derby County indulged in another display of their own unabashed benevolence and inexplicable incompetence by gifting victory to moderate opponents.' Quite kind by the standards of vitriol I seemed to have set myself. Remarkably,

20,625 turned up on the last day of the season to see Jimmy Armfield lead Blackpool to the easiest of 3-1 victories against a Derby team containing only three survivors of the Tim Ward era. Peter Taylor had almost got what he had said he wanted eight months earlier – a completely new team – yet the Rams had finished eighteenth, one place lower than the previous season. Clough's single cautious prediction – that the team would move up the table if only by one place – had proved wrong. So what happened in the aftermath of this horror story? Derby County sold a record number of season tickets.

Would the fans have been so keen, I wonder, had one of Clough and Taylor's more outrageous transfer plots come to fruition? That season had not been a great one for Kevin Hector. He had played well at times, but Taylor in particular was often frustrated by Kevin's lack of impact in games he felt he should have dominated. 'There's no devil in him,' he said one morning about halfway through that first season as we set off on our ritual stroll round the Baseball Ground pitch. 'I keep telling Brian, but he won't have it.' But Taylor was good at nagging when he thought he was right and as the weeks went by Cloughie started to come round to Pete's point of view and inevitably the same name would then crop up. 'With Waggy in this side we'd be in the top six. He'd get 30 goals a season,' said Peter, intensely irritated after one ineffective Derby performance and by now Clough was nodding every time Taylor jumped on this particular hobby horse and raised the name of one of his favourite players. Ken Wagstaff formed with Chris Chilton one of the best attacking spearheads in the country and to this day remains by some distance the most popular player in Hull City's history. Where Kevin Hector at his best would glide gracefully through defences, often running from deep, Wagstaff was a pugnacious, combative little bundle of energy, a rubber ball of a player who came to life in and around the opposition penalty area, all elbows and knees, awkward, with sharp reflexes and almost impossible to knock off the ball. Critics said too many of Wagstaff's many goals went in off his backside, 'but they sometimes said the same about me,' said Clough. 'If the ball goes in the net, that's all that matters.' Hector was in demand at the time. He was recognised as a brilliant player and there were several First Division sides who would have signed him, but Clough's first plan was to try to do a straight exchange deal – Wagstaff for Hector. Not surprisingly Hull would not contemplate this, nor were they remotely interested in talking about a fee for their best player. It would have been like Derby County selling, well, Kevin Hector. But getting Wagstaff had become something of an obsession and at this point Clough and Taylor's thinking became almost bizarre. I am assuming they had tapped Waggy up because they started to talk about getting him to go on strike and paying his wages themselves. For weeks they tried every trick they could think of, but in the end they accepted that Wagstaff was going nowhere and that they would have to depend on Hector to get them their goals. A couple of years later when Derby were rampaging through the First Division, with Hector consistently magnificent, I asked Taylor whether he still wished he could have done the Wagstaff swap. 'Absolutely,' he said. 'No question.' We will never know what Wagstaff might have achieved had he played in that wonderful Derby team, but we can be very certain that had that exchange deal gone through, supporters in Hull and Derby would have been outraged in equal measure.

CHAPTER 8

ENTER DAVE MACKAY

A few years ago, when a panel of four high-profile football figures came together on Sky TV to choose their all-time British post-war football team, the discussion started predictably enough. They chose their goal-keeper (Gordon Banks, I think, perhaps Peter Shilton), then after a long debate came up with a back four. So who, they were next asked, would play in midfield? No automatic choices there, surely? The assembled experts glanced at one another and there was much mutual nodding. 'Dave Mackay' said Tommy Docherty. 'Dave Mackay' said the three others, almost as one. 'Mackay?' asked the young presenter, 'was he really that good?' Docherty, already fairly florid by nature, turned almost scarlet with indignation. He and his fellow panellists were practically out of their seats. This was, it seemed, rather like asking a panel of opera buffs whether Maria Callas could carry a tune. Mackay, they assured this startled young man, was a truly great player who would have been great in any era, and this was the same Dave Mackay I met for the first time at the front counter of the Baseball Ground in July 1968. It was almost impossible to grasp. The legendary Mackay, a giant of the game who in his prime would have walked into any football team in the world, had signed for Derby County. I suspect I was completely overawed and all I can really remember of our interview was his 'nice little club' remark that has since been quoted so often. In cold print it might have seemed patronising at the time, but it did not come across that way at all. It was simply an honest view of how Derby County seemed to him on first acquaintance. He was softly spoken, matter of fact, almost downbeat with not a hint of swagger or arrogance, but you knew straight away that when he said something he meant it and I remember walking back to the office feeling a sense of excitement. It was an excitement that swept through the town. Nothing during the entire Clough–Taylor era had such an astonishing impact on the club's supporters as that one simple announcement – 'Derby County have signed Dave Mackay.'

That this announcement was made first in the *Derby Evening Telegraph* owed nothing to my abilities as a digger-out of exclusives and everything to Brian Clough's commitment to keeping our bargain. You play fair by me, he had said, and I will play fair by you. Yet even allowing for his determination to keep this sensational transfer quiet for several hours it was remarkable that the news did not get out. I had no idea that Clough and Taylor had hatched a plot to bring Mackay to the Baseball Ground. After all, though the Derby press corps had by now become used to signings coming out of the blue, none of the new faces so far had been a big name. Like others, I had read that Mackay was likely to bring his distinguished career with Tottenham Hotspur to an end and head off to his first club, Hearts, where the player-manager's job awaited him. It never crossed my mind that even Cloughie would do something quite so audacious as to try to sign Mackay for Derby. Then came a mid-afternoon telephone call from Vic Railton, the chief football writer on the *London Evening News*. Vic, who had extraordinary contacts in London, always seemed to be in a permanent state of feverish excitement, babbling away at 100 miles an hour in the broadest of broad East London accents, and so it was on this occasion: 'Did you know Cloughie's in London? He's just been spotted in a white Rolls-Royce on the North Circular Road.' This sounded most unlikely. I pointed out that Clough did not have a white Rolls-Royce and so far I knew he was at the Baseball Ground because I had spoken to him that morning. But Vic wanted me to check so I rang the ground, got through to Taylor and asked if I could have a word with Brian.

'Not here,' said Pete. 'Won't be in till the morning.'

'Not to worry I'll try him at home. Will he be there yet?'

There was no reply from an unusually reticent Taylor, which in its way was encouraging, so I went for the more direct approach.

'I heard he was in London. Anything going on?'

It was fairly obvious Peter didn't quite know where to go from here. There was a pause, then, 'has he said anything to you?' to which I could only reply 'about what?' but I was quick to add that nothing he told me could scupper any transfer because our last edition had printed, so the next story we published would be the following day. Reassured by this, Peter rather reluctantly admitted Brian was in London, 'but I can't tell you where or why, Brian will have to tell you himself,' then as ever could not keep his excitement to himself, adding, 'but if it comes off it will be a big one.' Now it was my turn to be reluctant because I had to ring Vic Railton back and I didn't really want the story – whatever that story might turn out to be – to appear in the early edition of the next day's *London Evening News* which was on the streets before nine o'clock in the morning. It would be picked up by the BBC and on the radio and TV news long before the *Derby Telegraph* was in the shops. So it was perhaps as well that I did not have the faintest clue why Clough was in London. I levelled with Vic, explaining that while his tip-off had been spot on (the Rolls-Royce must have been Sam Longson's), I could get no further at my end. And that was how we left it with Vic, whose usually good contacts could not come up with the goods, convinced that Brian was at Highbury. In the end, thanks to an early-morning call from Clough, I was able to ring Vic and put him out of his misery. He was as delighted as I was because, thanks to a pact between Clough and Spurs manager Bill Nicholson, not a line had appeared in any national morning paper. Early the previous evening Mackay had agreed to leave Tottenham and head for the unglamorous lower reaches of the Second Division and somehow it was all kept quiet for more than twelve hours.

Mackay had made his name in the great Tottenham side of the early 1960s, when he and Danny Blanchflower, the two wing halves, were the fulcrum of the side and it was perhaps because Blanchflower was always remembered for his wonderful skills that Mackay has since been categorised by some as a simply a hard man. Nothing could be further from the truth. Mackay was certainly as hard a player as ever went into a tackle – who can forget the iconic photograph of him grabbing a terrified-looking Billy Bremner by the front of his shirt and practically lifting him off the ground – but to write him off as nothing more than a tough nut, a Ron Harris or a Peter Storey, does him far less than justice, because he would have been world-class had he been no more physical than Ossie Ardiles. He had great balance, marvellous skills and a poise on the ball that made him a joy to watch. He turned the simple act of kicking the ball into something approaching an art form and when my former colleague Gerald Mortimer said it was worth the admission fee to any game just to see Dave kicking in before the start he could not have put it better. He had everything and would be almost beyond price in today's game.

For all that skill, Mackay will be remembered most fondly at Derby for the sheer level of inspiration he brought to the club and the self-belief he subsequently gave the side. 'You did quite often get the feeling that with Dave in the team you just couldn't lose,' Alan Hinton once said. 'When things were going wrong you just had to look across at him, fist clenched urging everybody on. He just had an amazing effect.' That effect spread from the pitch and around the terraces. When Mackay led the team out it sometimes seemed that barrel chest arrived on the field a couple of seconds before the rest of him. He exuded confidence and authority as well he might given his extraordinary gifts. Though older than Clough and with a football CV to match any in the game, I never recall Mackay trying to take advantage of his manager, his admirable professionalism illustrated perfectly by something that happened before a midweek evening game at Crystal Palace for which Clough, always on the look-out for something different, decided to prepare by taking the team to Bisham Abbey, the sports complex near the Thames in Buckinghamshire. We set off from Derby fairly early, the plan being for the players to have a meal then go to bed for a couple of hours in the afternoon and Dave, who had been down at his home in London for a couple of days, was scheduled to meet us there. We duly lunched and the players went for a short stroll before disappearing to lie down for an hour or two. All the players except Dave Mackay, that is. There was no sign of him at all and Clough was getting agitated. By two o'clock he was pacing up and down looking at his watch and half an hour later cursing not exactly under his breath and probably becoming concerned that there might have been some sort of accident. 'Where the hell's the skipper?' he asked Taylor two or three times in ten minutes, rather pointlessly since Peter obviously had no more idea than he did. This was, of course, long before the days of mobile phones, so I volunteered to go along to the reception desk and ask whether there had been any message from a Mr Dave Mackay. 'Mr Mackay arrived at around 11a.m. and went straight to his room,' I was told. 'He has asked to be called at 3.30 and not be disturbed before then.' End of a mini-crisis and any suggestion that Dave Mackay might have let his standards drop. Cloughie still managed to look faintly cross, but he was clearly very relieved. Though Dave never exploited his status there were times when he used it, but always in an entirely positive way. One

Monday morning the debrief from the previous Saturday's game went on longer than usual and it was not a happy gathering. Clough had laid into the players non-stop, complaining about anything and everything and rounding off by thrusting an arm towards Willie Carlin and saying, 'You should all give your wages to Willie this week. The little bugger carried you on his shoulders for ninety minutes.' There was an uncomfortable silence before the chastened players filed out for the usual game of five-a-side, Clough following on behind. 'Right then,' said Mackay when they got on to the pitch, gathering some of the players round him, 'no five-a-side today. It's the rest of us against Willie.' I am sure Clough laughed as much as the players. Tension over. Normal business resumed. Very much the assured, intuitive Mackay touch.

Clough admired everything about Dave Mackay, his skill, temperament, leadership and warrior qualities. 'He inspires me just as much as he inspires the rest of the team,' he would say. 'Bill Nicholson told me that with six Dave Mackays in your team you wouldn't need anybody else. I sometimes think five would do it.' The fee Derby paid for him, just £5,000, was nothing more than a gesture, but Mackay was an expensive acquisition, because he became the best paid player in the country. His pay of £250 a week seems laughably modest today, but throw in bonuses and he earned around £16,000 in his first season, which was more than First Division stars like George Best and Bobby Moore. And, being Derby County, they had to find a way of paying him which was not within the rules. When I was asked to ghost a column for Dave in the Derby County programme I happily agreed to do it. It gave me a chance to chat to him on a regular basis and we would meet for a natter in the bar at the Midland Hotel, where he lived when he was in Derby, then I would knock out a couple of hundred words on what ever topic we had agreed. Nothing could be easier and the pay, £3 an article, was not something I could afford to turn down. Little did I know, however, that Dave's pay for this column was rather more than £3. How big a chunk of his salary was paid this way I am not sure, certainly a substantial proportion, but whatever it was it bent the rules and was one of the contributory factors to the financial mess at the Baseball Ground which later led to the Rams being banned from Europe. Not a scrap of blame for this could be laid at the door of Dave Mackay, the man who did so much to get Derby into Europe in the first place. But the club paid a heavy price for trying to be too clever.

CHAPTER 9

WILLIE AND LES

There is a tendency for people to lump footballers together – a typical footballer, as in a typical politician, typical publican, perhaps even a typical traffic warden – and it is true that these days the best soccer players have a lot in common, largely because they all earn huge amounts of money, enabling them all to have big houses and expensive cars, in addition to which they seem six-footers at least. It was not always like that, at least not where Brian Clough's teams were concerned. He wanted players with real character and that inevitably meant that he was prepared to sign one or two who did not conform to any stereotype. Two of those he took to Derby became the nearest thing to cult figures that Brian's own ego would ever allow and both were fascinating men and, in some respects, the most unlikely footballers. In any poll to decide the best signing Brian Clough and Peter Taylor made for Derby County, the names of Dave Mackay and Roy McFarland would probably head the list; one a seasoned world-class legend, the other a brilliant youngster, both of whom gave the club magnificent service. Yet arguably the most crucial signing was that of a tough little scouser, who arrived in bizarre circumstances to provide the essential ingredient the team lacked. For all the disappointments of the previous season, there was huge optimism in Derby in the summer of 1968. Clough had, after all, signed Mackay, so what could possibly go wrong? In fact, initially nothing did go significantly wrong, but not enough went right either. Derby opened up with a 1-1 draw at Blackburn which would almost certainly have been a heavy defeat but for an inspired goalkeeping display by Les Green, then the level of that almost blind optimism was confirmed when 24,760, the biggest crowd of the day in the Second Division, turned up at the Baseball Ground to watch another 1-1 draw, this time with Blackpool. But if that was all slightly deflating, far worse was to follow. The Rams went to Bramall Lane where they were outplayed and lost 2-0 to Sheffield United, then on to Huddersfield where they were again on the end of a 2-0 defeat. This was not good news and there were certainly mutterings in the boardroom and probably on the terraces, too, but something special was just round the corner.

Willie Carlin, who had inspired Sheffield United to that 2-0 victory over Derby – and scored a brilliant goal – had not been at Sheffield long and was in the process of buying a house, so when he was called to Bramall Lane after training he assumed it was to talk about his mortgage. His manager John Harris had news for him – 'yes we can sort out your mortgage if you decide to stay here, but I have to tell you Brian Clough is in the next room. He wants to talk to you.' Carlin was not a happy man. Having only just arrived at the club he did not want to uproot his family again so soon, so at first refused point blank even to see Clough ('I thought it was a set-up. I just wanted to get the mortgage organised then go home,' he said later), but for his own reasons, whatever they may have been, Harris insisted, partly on the grounds that it would be bad manners to turn Clough away without even listening to him. So Carlin reluctantly agreed and, once exposed to Cloughie's talent for painting vivid pictures of his dream for Derby County, began to weaken, at least to the point when he said he would go home and discuss the whole business with his wife. Clough protested vigorously, playing the 'who wears the trousers in your house?' card, but Willie was adamant, so Clough changed tactic. 'Right, where are you staying?' he said. 'Let's go and see what your wife says. My car.' And within seconds Willie found himself being marched out of the ground and into the passenger seat of Brian's Rover. A few minutes later Carlin walked through his front door with Clough close behind. 'Do you want to move to Derby?' he asked his wife Marie. 'Now or tomorrow?' came the rather startling response and that was enough of an invitation for Clough, who straight away went into overdrive. 'He talked to her about carpets, curtains, furniture, the kids. I might as well not have been there,' said Willie afterwards. 'Eventually I had to butt in and say "hey, it's me you're signing, not my missus" but by then it was all over.' The next day Carlin travelled to Derby to sign and it was only when he left the Baseball Ground to get the train back to Sheffield that he thought to buy a paper and see where his new club stood in the table. 'I was stunned. They had two points from four games, Sheffield United had won every game and were top. For a minute I wondered what I had let myself in for.' He had no need to worry. Carlin, all five feet three inches of him, was the final piece in the Clough and Taylor jigsaw. He never looked back and neither did Derby County.

Carlin had been a brilliant footballer from early childhood and though small even for a youngster, was capped by England at schoolboy level. Manchester United were keen on him, but while still only fifteen he found himself signed up by Blackburn Rovers, whose manager Johnny Carey had blatantly broken the rules to get him to sign a form tying him to the club until he left school. Young Willie's chance for escape came when he begged a lift back from Blackburn to his Merseyside home on the Liverpool team coach after a midweek game and was asked what plans he had when he left school. When he said he was definitely not going to join Blackburn he was quickly made an offer he was not going to refuse and agreed to move to Anfield. His height, or lack of it, was always against him, but even more so was the refusal of his parents to allow him to turn full-time professional. As he recalled later:

> They wanted me to complete an apprenticeship, which was fair enough because there was no guarantee I was going to make the grade, but Liverpool had almost fifty professionals on the staff at that time and even though I was playing for the reserves when I was sixteen and a half I knew my chances were disappearing.

He did Liverpool one massive favour, however, by persuading one of his old school mates to join him there: 'I asked him over and over again to come down with me and have a trial but for ages he kept making excuses until I eventually got him to the ground and he had his trial and signed.' A massive favour? The lad he dragged to Anfield was Ian Callaghan, who went on to make 857 first-team appearances, still a Liverpool record.

Carlin eventually became a full-timer but his moment had gone and opportunities were limited, so he moved from the grandeur of Anfield to the rather more primitive surroundings of The Shay, home of Halifax Town, where he learned the game at grassroots level. After two seasons of being kicked from pillar to post – and kicking quite a few back – he jumped at the chance to join Carlisle United, then a decent Second

Division side and it was there he first came to the attention of Clough and Taylor when they were with Hartlepool. Inevitably his lack of inches was not the slightest consideration when they weighed up what he had to offer. They saw a tough, combative and skilful player who was frightened of nobody, could get a goal, read a game superbly and who battled away from home just as much as he did in front of his own supporters. Once installed at Derby, they soon made him a target, but it was not to be straightforward. Carlisle had appointed Tim Ward as manager, the man who had been sacked by Derby County not long before, and there was absolutely no way he was going to let his best player join the club who had so recently shown him the door. Strategy was called for and Peter Taylor was the man who rang Carlin at home to tap him up. 'Go and see Tim Ward,' Taylor told him. 'Tell him you want First Division football and then sit tight until I get back to you.' Willie did just that and a few days later Taylor was back on the telephone – 'right, we've made a bid for you. Go and see Tim again and ask him if there have been any offers.' Tim Ward, an inherently decent man, was honest. No offers at all, he said to Willie, 'you want First Division football and no First Division clubs have come in for you,' then as he was leaving the office, 'there has been an offer from the Second Division, but you won't want to go there, they're absolute rubbish.' Willie turned back and asked who this rubbish team were. 'Derby County,' replied Ward, who had been managing Derby eighteen months earlier and seen his former club subsequently sign O'Hare, Hinton, McFarland and Mackay. Rubbish was perhaps not the most accurate description. Ward, good fellow though he was, would not let Clough talk to Carlin, even though Brian had made it clear that he was prepared to top any other offer by £10,000, but Willie took the next exit opportunity like a shot and joined Sheffield United for £45,000. And that, he thought, was that, until twelve months later when Cloughie, never one to give up easily when in pursuit of a player, turned up and paid £63,000 for him – a thousand pounds an inch, as he was often reminded. Clough was ecstatic, though enraged and exasperated by one reaction. As Carlin ran out to make his debut a few days later, Brian overheard one director turn to another and say, 'how ridiculous. Fancy paying £63,000 for somebody that size.' The manager was not amused.

Willie Carlin became something of a folk hero. He was that rarity in sport – the little 'un who could take on and lick the big 'un, bouncing with confidence and afraid of nobody, so he quickly gained a reputation as a distinctly no-nonsense customer. One midwinter Saturday morning the Baseball Ground pitch was rock solid after a sharp frost, requiring the referee to arrive at the ground early to make sure the surface was playable, so I popped down for the inspection to find Willie emerging from the dressing room having had a spot of treatment just as the referee walked off the pitch.

'Is it OK, ref?' asked Willie.

'Yes, we'll play,' came the reply, 'and I don't want any trouble from you this afternoon or you'll be off.'

'Bloody hell,' said Willie as the referee walked off. 'I've had a warning already and we don't kick off for five hours.'

Willie Carlin was never beaten until the final whistle went. Not that he was beaten very often that season. After that inauspicious start Derby lost just two more League games, one of which Carlin missed (a 1-0 home defeat by Crystal Palace) and the other a 2-0 defeat at Crystal Palace when he played against medical advice with a large abscess on a knee. Willie could hardly raise a gallop that day and neither was he feeling much better when he turned up at the ground the following Thursday having been given a few days off to allow the abscess to heal only to discover the Baseball Ground practically deserted because Clough and Taylor had taken the players to Blackpool for a three-day break before their next scheduled game at Bloomfield Road. He was to follow on with directors Sam Longson and Sydney Bradley in Longson's Rolls-Royce in the hope he would be able to play and a little reluctantly he passed himself fit only to be smacked a fearful blow on the damaged knee after only five minutes. When Willie said afterwards that he did not touch the ball for the next eighty-five minutes he was more or less 100 per cent accurate, but if ever he proved his value to the side it was that day. He just walked and trotted round the middle of the field, shouting instructions, pointing and waving like a demented Italian traffic cop. Derby won 3-2 and when the players arrived back in the dressing room at the final whistle, Clough shook the exhausted Carlin by the hand and just said 'thanks Willie'. It was, said Carlin, the only time the manager ever shook his hand after a game, 'but that was the gaffer. He could make you feel a million dollars.' Willie Carlin would certainly be worth a lot more than a million dollars if he was playing today.

If Willie was small to be a midfielder at just five feet three inches, what price a goalkeeper who was five feet eight and a half, or maybe just about five feet nine with his boots on? These days, clubs rarely look at a 'keeper if he is not at least six feet tall, so nobody would give the time of day to a latter-day Les Green. Remarkable, then, that for two seasons Green was without doubt a match for any goalkeeper in the country. To be fair to Greenie he gave the impression of being much bigger than he was. Just as opposing forwards often said Peter Shilton always seemed about seven feet tall and three feet across, so Les Green somehow managed to convey a physical dominance that strictly speaking did not exist. He also had hands like dustbin lids and was an absolute master craftsman when it came to cutting angles, closing down attackers as they came at him and – perhaps most important of all – organising those in front of him. 'Basically I was a short-arse,' he said at one recent get-together of former players. 'I had to get the angles right and I had to time everything dead right. There was not any margin for error.' Green, like Carlin, took the long road to fame and there were many diversions along the way. He started out with Atherstone Town as a kid, then moved to Hull City but was homesick and soon returned to the Midlands to join Nuneaton Borough and it was there he was spotted by Peter Taylor, then managing Burton Albion. It was the start of a long and close relationship. 'Talking to Pete about football was like talking to Einstein about science,' Green was to say, prompting the unlikely picture of Les debating the theory of relativity with his brainy mate Albert in the back room of a Berlin pub. It was a fair analogy because Peter talked football, and goalkeeping in particular, as if it was a science. Green was a big success in the Southern League and when Taylor left to join Clough at Hartlepools he was soon back with a £2,000 cheque 'to put Les in the Football League where he belonged'. But before long there were problems – Green and Clough never truly saw eye to eye – and the upshot was that Green walked out and signed for Rochdale. So that, surely, was that. But it was not, because when it became clear that Reg Matthews' great career at Derby was coming to a close, Taylor was determined bygones should be bygones and a reconciliation was essential.

The 1967/68 season had just finished when Green received a phone call from Bob Stokoe, his manager at Rochdale. 'Your mate's been on the phone for you,' he said. 'Are you interested?' Les did not need to be told who this particular mate was. And off he went to Derby. 'Brian was not that keen, but so far as I was concerned Les was one of the best six goalkeepers in the country,' said Taylor. 'At that time all clubs seemed to regard goalkeepers as less important than outfield players which was crazy. You start by sorting out the spine of your side, goalkeeper, centre half, centre forward, and that is what we did – Green, McFarland, O'Hare.' Yes they did, but only after Clough relented and agreed to patch it up with a player he probably thought he would never employ again. It proved to be an inspired signing. Green made his debut in a 1-1 draw at Blackburn in which Derby were outplayed from start to finish and might well have lost by five goals or more had it not been for the brilliance of their new goalkeeper. Beaten only by a penalty (which he nearly saved) he made a series of astonishing saves and in ninety minutes swept away any doubt supporters might have had that some little fellow from Rochdale they had last heard of playing down the road for Burton Albion might not be up to the challenge. Throughout his time at Derby, Green never ceased to amaze and one save will live with all who watched the Rams thrash Tottenham Hotspur 5-0 at the Baseball Ground in early September 1969. Derby were winning 2-0 and playing superbly when Spurs broke away and after a brilliant counter-attack the ball was crossed to Jimmy Greaves, who was hovering maybe a yard or so back from the penalty spot. Greaves, side-on to the goal, took the ball on his thigh and as it dropped hammered a magnificent, beautifully struck shot towards the top left-hand corner. It looked a certain goal, but Green took off and not only got to the ball but held it in both hands. The crowd erupted while Greaves stood, hands on knees, mouth wide open. To his credit he actually applauded for a second or two, yet at half-time he found himself in trouble. Having somehow caught Greaves' shot, Green was immediately back on his feet and – a quick and brilliant distributor – hurled the ball to Alan Hinton on the left wing. Seconds later Derby had won a corner, which was headed in at the near post by Willie Carlin and Derby were 3-0 up. 'The Spurs defence were looking out for Roy McFarland coming in at the far post as usual, but when Alan placed the ball for the corner he glanced up and saw me just tap my forehead,' said Carlin. 'The corner came over and I did not have to move. That's how good Alan Hinton was.' Jimmy Greaves in trouble? When the players went in at half-time, their manager Bill Nicholson launched into his legendary striker, apparently complaining that 'if you had scored instead of mis-hitting that shot they wouldn't have broken away and it would be 2-1 now instead of 3-0.' Nicholson's reaction was surely a simple case of frustration because far from mis-hitting the shot Greaves caught it perfectly and it was going like a rocket. Dave Mackay, in his own autobiography, describes Green's save as the best he has ever seen, surpassing even Gordon Banks' fantastic stop from Pele's header in the 1970 World Cup, while Greaves told Les some time later that he had never been so certain a shot was going in. He had turned away half celebrating – 'then the next thing the ball is flying back over my head, Derby get a corner and we are 3-0 down.'

Les Green was a natural life-and-soul-of-the-party man with a kind of Freddie Starr off-the-wall sense of the ridiculous, but he was a fierce trainer always looking for ways to improve. He sees today's goalkeepers as out-and-out shot-stoppers and not a patch on his own generation, when the likes of Shilton, Ray Clemence and Pat Jennings were in their prime. Green was an automatic choice during a run of 129 consecutive appearances, organising the defence superbly ('the best in the game for that,' said Taylor) but it all fell apart when he had a nightmare in a 4-4 draw with Manchester United and was promptly dropped in favour of Colin Boulton. 'All of a sudden it all went wrong and that was more or less it between me and Derby County,' he said later. So why did it go wrong? There were off-the-field issues and Green freely admits that he had made some mistakes along the way. 'I might have made some errors of judgement away from the ground but when I was training and playing I was always 100 per cent committed,' he said, but this time it was well and truly over between him and Clough and their fall-out was not only final but so explosive that there was no chance they would ever kiss and make up again:

> After about six months of being mucked about and not knowing where I was with the club I went to Brian's office and told him I wanted to sort everything out face to face once and for all, but I chose the wrong time because he was knocking back the brandies. He shouted and swore at me to get out, so I shoved him and he fell off his chair. I just turned round and walked out.

Pushing Brian Clough off a chair is not a recommended career move and Green was soon on his way. It was a sad end to a fine career at the very top for a man who but for Taylor's perceptive eye might have spent all his days in the lower reaches of the Football League. Despite all that happened between them, Green remained an admirer of everything Clough achieved:

You can't take his record away from him and he was a great motivator. For a long time I thought the world of him and the way he and Peter played off each other was brilliant, but to say I was disappointed by his attitude when he no longer thought I was his best goalkeeper is putting it mildly. At that time he lost my respect completely.

He was also still angry and hugely disappointed that Clough had the previous year refused permission for him to make his mark at international level. Alf Ramsey was keen take Green on an England 'A' summer tour of Australia, but Clough would not agree on the grounds that he wanted his goalkeeper to rest when the season ended, something Les found especially galling when several of his teammates were allowed to play in the end-of-season home internationals. Green had, of course, always been a Taylor man, perhaps not surprisingly given the way Peter had moulded his career:

> So far as I am concerned Peter Taylor was a genius. He taught me a lot and he taught Brian a lot, too. He really was the brains and whenever things were not going right and they were trying to get us back on track it was Clough listening to Taylor, not the other way round. Peter never got the recognition he deserved. When they gave Brian the Freedom of Derby and then Nottingham they should have done just the same for Pete. So far as I am concerned that road between Derby and Nottingham should not be called Brian Clough Way, it should be Clough and Taylor Way.

It is easy to read bitterness into these remarks, but also hard to dispute that Taylor is already seen by many present-day football people as a bit-part player when, in fact, he was a genuine partner, whose contribution to the success of Derby County and Nottingham Forest was immense.

CHAPTER 10

PROMOTION AT A CANTER

So far as I know only two players ever went on record as saying they would never sign for Derby County. One was Lou Macari, who signed for Manchester United from Celtic rather than even consider a move to the Baseball Ground, and the other Graham Cross, a midfielder at Leicester City who Brian Clough tried to sign at the start of the 1968/69 season. Cross was a good player who would certainly have improved the Derby side, but after all sorts of behind-the-scenes wrangling, any hope of a deal disappeared, leaving Cross to say he would not sign for Derby if Clough crawled to Leicester and begged him and Clough saying that if Cross crawled to Derby he would not sign him anyway. Very strange, but in the end Cross was the loser. Where he would have played is anybody's guess, possibly in Alan Durban's midfield slot, but Cross must have had very mixed feelings as that season progressed, with Derby moving through the gears until they hit overdrive in March and April.

With Carlin slotted in as the final piece of the jigsaw, one look at the team sheet indicated that this was a side brimming with talent and, like the supporters, I could hardly wait to see what would happen once they settled down. Carlin made his debut in a scrappy 2-2 home draw against Hull City, Ken Wagstaff inevitably scoring one of Hull's goals, and it was perhaps a helpful piece of timing that the next game was a home League Cup tie against Stockport County, modest opposition unlikely to present much of a problem. Sure enough the players relaxed, Alan Hinton scored four times in a 5-1 romp and Derby County were up and running. It was almost as if somebody had flicked a switch.

Soon, after a 3-1 win over Aston Villa, I was able to write, 'Derby are now good enough to beat some Second Division sides without even playing very well,' and by the end of September I was even more upbeat: 'We are still waiting for the Rams to leave the field to a standing ovation, but who can be surprised that there is already promotion talk in the town?' Dave Mackay was by now in his element, completely at home in his new role as a sweeper and it was fascinating to watch his confidence rubbing off on his younger teammates. 'Who are we playing today?' he would ask on the way to an away match. 'Who have they got, anybody we've heard of?' It was not bravado, just great Dave Mackay psychology that could not fail to inspire his teammates. It was also obvious Mackay was enjoying every minute of it, 'grinning broadly and waving to the fans when he trotted off at the end as if his lifetime ambition had always been to get Derby County into the First Division,' I wrote after another victory. But this was only the start. After that League Cup victory over Stockport, Derby had been drawn away to Chelsea in the next round, so had a chance to test themselves against a very good First Division side bristling with internationals, and they did themselves proud. Mackay, back on the big stage at Stamford Bridge, was quite magnificent and a 0-0 draw was no more than the Rams deserved. Peter Taylor was beaming broadly afterwards, but Clough was surprisingly subdued. 'Should be some replay, Brian,' said somebody back at the hotel. Cloughie gave him a scowl. 'Saturday's game at Bolton is all I'm worried about at the moment,' was all he would say. As it turned out he had no need to worry, because the players had their feet firmly back on the ground three days later and won 2-1 at Bolton, where Jimmy Walker scored a brilliant individual goal, beating three men and cracking a terrific left-foot shot into the top corner, prompting Clough to leap from the dug-out and do a jig of delight on the touchline. And so the scene was set for what many would say was the Baseball Ground's greatest night, not just of that season, but any season.

The League Cup replay against Chelsea was one of those 'I was there' occasions, a never-to-be-forgotten epic and without question the most dramatic and exciting game of football I have ever seen. It was gripping from the start, Derby immediately playing with fluent brilliance, but it moved to another level from the twenty-sixth minute when Alan Birchenall put Chelsea into the lead completely against the run of play. As the players jogged back I looked across at Dave Mackay, who was hitching up his shorts and pursing his lips. At that moment he appeared to say nothing to his teammates, but the look on his face said it all. The game restarted and Derby simply launched themselves at the Chelsea defence. Mackay, chest out, jaw jutting as he drove his team forward, was unstoppable and the supporters, sensing they were witnessing something quite exceptional, caught the mood. The noise in the ground was extraordinary as attack followed attack and Chelsea's aristocrats were reduced to belting the ball anywhere. The volume went up again. A relentless 'Derby, Derby' chant rolled round the ground, creating an atmosphere which prompted one veteran supporter to say years later that it was the nearest thing he could imagine to a Nuremburg rally. An unfortunate comparison, perhaps, but looking back it was easy to see what he meant because this was raw passion elevated to fever pitch. Chelsea were on their knees and in the seventy-first minute the dam burst. Willie Carlin raced through the middle as Chelsea back-pedalled, then suddenly back-heeled the ball into the path of – who else? – Dave Mackay, who struck a magnificent twenty-five-yarder into the top corner. The roar might almost have been heard back in Tottenham and not one person in the crowd would have put a button on Chelsea coming back from that. Alan Durban headed a second from Jimmy Walker's cross and with something close to hysteria engulfing the terraces Kevin Hector grabbed a third. When the final whistle went and the players threw their arms aloft in triumph, the crowd erupted and none of us were in any doubt that this emerging Derby team could ultimately achieve greatness. Mackay could by now have been at Hearts, Walker still at Northwich, Green at Rochdale and O'Hare at Sunderland. McFarland might have been at Tranmere, Carlin with Sheffield United, Robson playing junior football in the north-east, Hinton languishing in Forest's reserves. But all were at the Baseball Ground in company with the three great survivors from the Tim Ward era, Durban, Hinton and Ronnie Webster. And what a night they gave us.

Derby was buzzing. Football seemed the only topic and people who had not been to the Baseball Ground for years suddenly rediscovered their enthusiasm. I seemed to be working morning, noon and night, seven days a week, but it hardly seemed like work. Being in the thick of this was just wonderful and I found it almost impossible to go anywhere without being bombarded by questions from supporters, so I can't begin to imagine what it must have been like for the players. The bandwagon continued to roll and there was much excitement when the Rams drew another First Division club in the next round of the League Cup. This time it was Everton, again it was away from home, and again the Rams defended well enough to earn a 0-0 draw and a replay. This was never going to match up to the Chelsea game and it didn't, but Derby won 1-0 and were starting to move within sight of the final. The fans were on a permanent high, often pouring into the ground an hour before the kick-off. What was going to happen next? Well in my case what happened was that I collapsed. Derby had beaten Birmingham City 1-0 on a miserably damp November afternoon and I was driving back up to my Matlock home early in the evening when I heard a bang as my exhaust pipe hit the road. I drove an ancient Mini so this was no surprise and as I kept a piece of rope in the back for just such an emergency, I was soon home. But no sooner had I walked through the door than I blacked out, keeled over and came round a few seconds later with a blinding headache and tears streaming down my face. Our doctor was a family friend and he was round within a few minutes. He laid the law down almost Clough-style. I was overdoing it, he said, and the little incident with the exhaust pipe had just been the final straw. 'You're a fit young man,' he told me, 'but if anything like this happens again you'll be off work for three months.' As it was he told me to take a week off. There was to be no medication – 'but walk up to the Sycamore on Wednesday or Thursday and have a couple of pints of Guinness. Go back to work a week on Monday but stop trying to do too much. You can't go on working seven days a week.' The Sycamore was our local and I think I brought my date with the Guinness forward by a couple of days.

I rang my deputy David Moore the following day to put him in the picture. Derby were playing Swindon in the next round of the League Cup on the Wednesday, then were due at Bury three days later and he would have to cover both, while I put my feet up for a few days. If only. The Swindon game duly came and went, a poor 0-0 draw, but on the Friday the *Telegraph*'s editor 'Mac' McInnes rang full of apologies with just the news I didn't want. David Moore had flu and could not get out of bed, so was there any way I could cover the Bury game. Naturally I protested at first, but eventually agreed and rang Brian Clough. 'What time is the bus leaving for Bury?' I asked. The reply was the one I might have expected – 'What the bloody hell are you talking about? I thought you were supposed to be ill.' When I explained that Dave Moore was sick there was a short pause, then 'We'll pick you up at ten o'clock. See you tomorrow.' And down went the telephone. There was surely something wrong here, because when the Rams went up to Lancashire the route was always the same – Derby, Ashbourne, Leek, Macclesfield for lunch then on to the match, but not this time. Brian had been to our house on several occasions so knew how to find it and sure enough just before 10a.m. the coach pulled up outside, Cloughie having arranged a considerable detour to save me having to go the twenty miles to Derby. Half an hour or so into the journey he plonked himself down next to me and handed me an envelope – 'You and your wife go and have a few days away. You look like a bloody old man.' The envelope contained a holiday voucher which would have paid for a very nice trip abroad, but obviously I could not accept it. 'Fair enough,' he said, stuffing the envelope into his pocket and the subject was never mentioned again. Meanwhile it had started to pour with rain and by the time we reached Bury the pitch was waterlogged. After all that the match was postponed.

Normal service was resumed on the Monday and two nights later, in a replay at Swindon, Derby went out of the League Cup to a fluke goal, a shot by Don Rogers hitting John Robson on the shoulder, spinning high into the air and dropping just under the bar. Derby, who were without John O'Hare and Alan Hinton that night, never really got going and Clough was in philosophical mood and decided to have a few beers. So, too, did several of the players and it must have been around three in the morning when we all crawled off to bed. Looking round the coach next morning, I was obviously not the only person not enjoying the journey home along those winding Wiltshire roads. Clough and Taylor – Peter especially it seemed to me – had shrugged off the previous night's defeat by the time we had got back to Derby. More League Cup glory would have been very acceptable and provided useful extra revenue, but the clear target was promotion and that was now the only focus. Momentum soon returned, in part brought about by the introduction into the side of John McGovern, who made his debut against Charlton Athletic the following Saturday in a 1-0 win. I appear to have been impressed, reporting on the Monday, 'not a lot of pace, but attacks rarely broke down with him because of his ability to play the ball with either foot. Did the right thing when he didn't have time to think, which is always a good sign.' And that was pretty much the way he went on playing throughout his entire career.

Curiously, supporters had become remarkably hard to please, perhaps spoiled by some of the dazzling displays earlier in the season. Some actually booed and jeered that win over Charlton, which considering it moved the side to second in the table, a point behind the leaders with a game in hand, seemed churlish by any standards or 'lamentable' as I wrote at the time – 'no wonder one or two of the players enjoy away matches more than home games.' Clough, though clearly irritated, took perhaps a rather more mature view when this was put to him, pointing out that the crowd was more than 25,000, 'and if they didn't like what we were doing there wouldn't be half that number.' Nonetheless the Baseball Ground jitters continued. 'Derby County seem to approach home games with all the enthusiasm of a nervous first-year pupil awaiting an interview with the headmaster,' was my take on it after they had managed only a 3-3 home draw with Carlisle United, though I excused the skipper – 'but not Dave Mackay. Markeaton Park or Madrid, it would make no difference to him.' Although Taylor continued to be defiantly optimistic – 'we'll close the gates before the end of the season' – Clough had realised that something had to be done. We usually met for a Sunday lunchtime drink, when Brian was invariably in good form, relaxed and looking forward as always to sitting down for the family lunch he enjoyed so much, but on this occasion he was unusually preoccupied, almost subdued. 'We're off the boil. We need a striker,' he said. 'And what's more I know who I want. He's just the man for this club.' I was surprised – 'You scored three yesterday and let three in, why a striker?' Clough saw the home-games complex as being entirely down to confidence. As he pointed out, the players were the same ones who had beaten Chelsea out of sight, but some had become afraid to try things in case they made mistakes and he felt one more strong character in the tiny first-team squad would make a big difference. On top of that, while there was a degree of cover in defence, there would be real problems were O'Hare and Hector to be injured at the same time.

I duly reported that Clough was trying to sign a striker, a story which caused much excitement and speculation among supporters judging from the correspondence and telephone calls we received. Another big name, they doubtless assumed, or perhaps a promising youngster, while I was wondering whether they might finally land Ken Wagstaff. In the event the outcome was slightly tame, because the man Clough brought in was Frank Wignall, a proven goalscorer but one generally thought to be past his best. And where would he play? Peter Taylor answered that one – 'with a bit of luck he won't play at all.' This was typical Clough–Taylor logic. Perhaps they thought the O'Hare–Hector partnership needed geeing up a bit or that one of them could do with a rest, but either way 'Big Frank' – and he was big – was to spend most of his time sitting on the bench. Wignall was a man of few words and minimalist habits. The first time we picked him up for an overnight away trip there was no sign of a bag or suitcase when he climbed on to the coach. 'Where's your bag, Frank? We're stopping over,' shouted Cloughie from one of the card tables towards the back of the coach, whereupon Frank put his hand into the inside pocket of his jacket and produced a toothbrush which he brandished flamboyantly to the huge amusement of his new teammates. Obviously a man who liked to travel light.

It cannot have been coincidence that performances and results started to improve. On Boxing Day Peter Taylor's 'we'll close the gates' prophecy all but came true when 34,481 watched the Rams beat Middlesbrough 3-2 to go three points clear at the top of the table and from then onwards confidence flowed back into the side. Brian and Peter had done it between them and Clough played another masterstroke at Bury, where after only twenty minutes Dave Mackay was felled by a flailing elbow which caught him on the temple and knocked him cold. Logic said the substitute should come on, but Clough was happy to play with ten men until half-time to see whether Mackay was fit enough to return, something which was not lost on the rest of the team, the crowd, or the Bury players. This was not arrogance, just Clough showing total faith in his players. As it turned out Mackay was not remotely well enough to play on and John McGovern moved to the sweeper role where he played with unexpected brilliance, helping Derby to win 1-0. By now the Rams were as good as unstoppable and the only panic was a personal one on the way to Birmingham. The team had travelled the day before (an overnight stop at Burton-on-Trent!), so I drove down to St Andrews only for that rogue exhaust pipe to fall off again when I was about three miles from the ground. Reasonably fit, I ran the rest of the way, getting into the press box about five minutes before the kick-off. Those critical supporters had by now long been silenced and by the time Derby beat Cardiff City 2-0 the crowd – 34,589 – was the third highest in the country behind those at Liverpool and Arsenal. What were the crowds going to be like the following season when, barring a catastrophic collapse, the likes of Liverpool and Arsenal would be coming to Derby? Not that anybody thought for a second that the Rams were suddenly going to fall apart. Any tension evaporated and the talk in the pubs was no longer constrained by ifs and buts, but of trips to Old Trafford, Highbury and St James's Park.

There will be some supporters who can still reel off the results of the famous 11-match unbeaten run-in at the end of the season, which started after that surprise midweek 1-0 home defeat by Crystal Palace when Willie Carlin was injured. The following morning Clough announced that they were off to Blackpool that day – 'to relax and enjoy ourselves before Saturday's game,' and that was just what they did, although Dave Mackay's idea of relaxing was to take over a table football machine. 'He came off after about two hours dripping with sweat,' said Clough. 'He just wouldn't let anybody beat him but we all know that's the way he is.' Mackay had recovered sufficiently from this unorthodox training session to lead Derby to a 3-2 win at Blackpool, then play outstandingly again in a 1-1 draw at Carlisle, where Paddy Ryan, the Rams' captain back in the Harry Storer days, had his first look at the new Derby County. Paddy, never one for wild exaggeration, was in raptures afterwards, describing John O'Hare's performance as astonishing. 'I could have sat and watched them all night and how it finished 1-1 I'll never know. Derby could have had eight.' Clough agreed – 'the only time they got the ball was when it went out of play,' he said with a rather self-satisfied smile.

By now London was starting to take note. After they had beaten Huddersfield 1-0, then strolled to a 2-0 win at Oxford, Brian Glanville wrote in the *Sunday Times* that Derby were 'arguably one of the best Second Division sides since the war', but neither these results nor Glanville's assessment impressed Tommy Docherty, the new manager of Aston Villa, who were to be the Rams' next opponents. Docherty took his team to Majorca for four days by way of preparation and returning proclaiming that 'all Derby County will get at Villa Park is a cup of tea'. On match day he was at his bumptious best – or worst depending on your point of view – insisting on walking round the touchline before kick-off milking the applause of the 50,000 crowd, but that was as good as it got for the Doc. He then had to sit and watch his team completely outplayed, Derby scarcely moving out of third gear as they coasted to a 1-0 victory, the entire 50,000 crowd (Derby supporters apart) having been reduced to silence long before the end. Only a cup of tea? 'Derby

County don't deal in cups of tea these days anyway,' I wrote the following Monday. 'Not when there's champagne on ice.'

And so it went on – a 1-0 win at Fulham then promotion secured
with a 5-1 Baseball Ground romp against Bolton Wanderers. 'First phase
completed,' said Clough, surprisingly quiet afterwards. 'Some people will
say we will come straight back down, but then they said we would go
down this season after we had only got three points from five games.'
Sheffield United were dispatched 1-0, and how sweet that must have
been for Willie Carlin, Millwall beaten 1-0 at the Den, then Norwich
thrashed 4-1 at Carrow Road, the Rams' fifth consecutive away win.
And so Bristol City arrived as sacrificial lambs on the final day of the
season, a beautiful late spring day, the ground full well over an hour
before the start. The City players jogged on to the pitch at 2.55p.m. to
find their opponents enjoying a lap of honour which they could only
stand and watch and indeed they seemed to be standing and watching
for the following ninety minutes as the Rams cruised home 5-0. Alan
Durban scored three times in the first half and so complete was Derby's
domination that McFarland, who had already hit the bar twice, could
have had a hat-trick from centre half in the second. It was just exhibition
stuff. This team was far, far too good for the Second Division.

Cloughie relaxed one of his firmest rules afterwards when he invited
me into the dressing room afterwards for a glass of champagne. Pride
and pleasure oozed out of him, and Taylor too, come to that. Where
Brian was always emotional by nature, Peter usually tended to keep his
feelings to himself, but even he was hugging people. As to what we all
did in the evening I have absolutely no idea, but I am fairly sure we
didn't go straight home.

That 11-game run-in, in which Derby scored 25 goals, conceded only
three (one a penalty) and finished with nine consecutive victories, five
away from home, was not the most remarkable aspect of that memorable season. What was truly amazing is that just twelve players effectively
achieved all this. Seventeen played in all but of these five played only 21
games between them. Unless a player was injured or ill then the team
picked itself, the only significant change being the introduction of John
McGovern to replace Jimmy Walker halfway through the season. Today
such a thing would be unthinkable.

CHAPTER 11

TRIUMPH AND DISAPPOINTMENT

Derby County supporters summered contentedly in 1969, still on a high after that breathtaking farewell to the Second Division, but there was no real close season for me, because the sales figure of the *Derby Telegraph* was at that time buoyed day after day by news from the Baseball Ground. Years later, Nottingham Forest supporters joked about Brian Clough walking on the River Trent, but so far as Rams fans were concerned Clough and Peter Taylor had mastered the art of walking on water years before on the Derwent. As I remember it, Brian spent much of the summer with his family. He also walked a lot, played a bit of squash and drank only in moderation. He was still a young man and, dodgy knee apart, a strikingly fit one. He and Peter were obviously looking forward to the new season though not obsessed by it, at least that was the impression they gave, but my job was to drum up news so I practically made camp at the Baseball Ground and thought everything was going smoothly until it emerged that neither Brian nor Peter had signed the new contracts they had been promised. Surely they were not being head-hunted already? In fact, the reason they had not signed was that no contracts had actually been drawn up, an extraordinary oversight for which Sydney Bradley, by then the chairman, took responsibility, adding, 'these contracts are currently being worked upon by the finest lawyers in Derby,' a splendidly grandiose statement that prompted many a wry smile. When this story broke I was away with the Rams in Holland for a pre-season game in Maastricht, where Clough responded to this casual incompetence by saying that, 'if I took as long to do my job as the

directors have to sort this out Derby County would be in rack and ruin.'
He was duly quoted on the front page of the paper, giving us a foretaste
of what was to come four years later.

Such was the upbeat mood in Derby as the new season approached
that this minor spat was soon forgotten, at least by the supporters. All they
were concerned about was that nothing should prevent them turning up
at the Baseball Ground at three o'clock on 9 August for the first game
of the new season against Burnley, though the gate as it turned out was
'only' 29,459, perhaps because some were on holiday. It was, of course, a
memorable occasion and I was as excited as any fan, but the match itself
was nothing special, a 0-0 draw notable mainly for a late penalty save by
Les Green, who dived the right way to beat away Frank Casper's kick,
explaining afterwards that he had seen Casper take penalties on television so knew which way to go. Football supporters are extraordinary
people and later that evening I heard several talking despondently about
how tough it was going to be, 'if we can't even win home games against
teams like Burnley', but I suspect they had cheered up again four days
later because the Rams extended their run of away wins (five at the
end of the promotion season) by winning 1-0 at Ipswich, where Roy
McFarland scored with a magnificent header from Alan Hinton's corner.
Ipswich was a club like no other in those days, the Cobbold family's
eccentric style making each visit there a delight. All and sundry seemed
to be allowed into the boardroom, not least the press contingent, who
took full advantage of 'Mr John's' liberal hospitality. No Baseball Ground
bottles of Bass for John. It was champagne or nothing and he didn't
approve of nothing. Rather unusually Peter Taylor came in for a drink,
but there was no sign of Brian who, said Peter, was tired and had gone to
sit on the bus. A further point was picked up at Coventry, where a Kevin
Hector 'winner' was disallowed because Willie Carlin was supposedly offside yards away, then the home faithfuls saw their first win when Ipswich
were beaten 3-1, a victory marred only by the sight of McFarland limping heavily with a groin injury he had picked up pre-season. It was an
injury he carried for months and he was not the only one who played
when far from fully fit, leading to accusations, almost certainly justified,
that Clough and Taylor would patch up their best players and push them
out on to the pitch whether it was good for their long-term well-being
or not. To the surprise of most of us, Cloughie then provided me with
a back-page lead in which he lambasted his players for not trying hard

enough and less than a week later, after a goalless draw with Stoke, he was at it again, hammering them for lack of effort, which seemed pretty tough after a five-game unbeaten start. I took a quite different approach and presumptuously wrote off most of the First Division, reporting, 'Derby could easily surprise a few this season because outside the top handful there is little to choose between the teams,' a rather sweeping conclusion in the third week of August, especially from somebody who had seen next to no First Division football.

The players were starting to find their feet, perhaps believing they were worthy of a place at football's top table. They drew at Wolves, then pulled off a 2-0 win at West Brom, a game notable for an outrageous spot of Carlin impudence. When Derby won a free-kick just outside the penalty area, Willie took it upon himself to orchestrate affairs and he was still urging the referee to take the West Brom wall further back when, without looking, he flicked the ball across to Dave Mackay who blasted it high into the net. The home players protested and I suspect these days the goal might have been disallowed, but on that occasion it stood, prompting Carlin to give the dug-out a grin and a thumbs-up as he trotted back to the halfway line. All of a sudden Derby were big news and the little press box at Derby was even more cramped than usual when the Rams faced their first big test of the new season against high-flying Everton. My optimism had evidently turned to realism, because I wrote before the game that Everton were in a different class to the sides the Rams had met so far and that the fans would be happy with a draw, but the usually cautious Clough was bursting with confidence when we had lunch before the game. Whether he and Peter had spotted something in Everton that suggested a weakness I don't know, but it is most unlikely because they never bothered to watch the opposition, so I can only assume it was something they had seen in their own players during the week. Either way they were right, Derby won 2-1, and my report the following Monday began, 'Derby County's remarkable, courageous ten-and-a-half (Roy McFarland is still not fully fit) first matched then outplayed Everton before an ecstatic almost disbelieving crowd. Only a series of great saves by Gordon West kept the score down.' Derby were indeed brilliant that day, cheered on by almost 38,000 roaring fans, who loved every minute, not least the way John McGovern reduced World Cup hero Alan Ball beyond frustration to impotent rage with a masterful display of man-to-man marking. I obviously lapped it up, too, clearly taking huge pleasure in writing, 'the third goal came after eight superb passes, not one of them backward, which left the team rated the best in Britain, baffled, bemused and beaten.' What I job I had in those days. I hope I appreciated it.

After a 3-0 win over Southampton, we all looked forward to a trip to Newcastle, nobody more than Cloughie, who was never happier than when back in the north-east. It was the first time I had ever been there and remember being surprised when, at about 10.30 on the Friday evening, Brian suggested we go out for a stroll and find somewhere for a bite to eat. At that time of night in the late 1960s, Derby would have been closing down, the last buses getting ready to take a few drinkers home to the suburbs, but Newcastle was alive with cafés, clubs and burger bars and there were people everywhere. What a place and how dreary Derby seemed by comparison. Derby had its own back the next afternoon, however, when the Rams silenced the massive St James's Park crowd. I sat about three seats away from the great Jackie Milburn, who was doing some reporting at the time but cared little for press-box conventions. He frequently leapt to his feet, berating players for their mistakes and urging the Newcastle side on whenever they attacked, which was not often, but even he went quiet eventually as bewitched as the rest of us as Newcastle were overwhelmed. 'It was like watching fish in a keep net, thrashing round and exhausting themselves,' I wrote of Newcastle's efforts to get into the game. At this point Clough and Taylor had become almost blasé in their approach, because McFarland was playing on one leg, Alan Hinton had a heavy cold and a dodgy thigh muscle, Alan Durban was limping with a bad knee and Les Green's bruised foot was so painful Dave Mackay was taking the goal kicks. Yet still Frank Wignall stayed on the bench. 'We maintained our rhythm so I left them as they were,' Clough said afterwards. 'I wanted Frank in reserve in case a defender was injured and John McGovern had to drop back.' When I climbed onto the coach ninety minutes or so after the final whistle for the journey home, Cloughie was sitting there staring at the front page of the Newcastle football paper, his eyes focused on the First Division table which showed Derby County at the top, unbeaten after 10 games, having conceded only four goals. Could even Brian believe it? I suspect we all had to pinch ourselves. Magical days turned into magical weeks and the season raced by.

We were all sucked into a curiously different world in which everybody even remotely associated with the club appeared to enjoy some sort of celebrity status. Indeed the whole of Derby seemed to start each day two or three gin and tonics to the good such was the mood. Clough and Taylor were by now regarded as Midas and Merlin, but as I saw it Brian still had his feet on the ground at this point, perhaps because Peter had his hands firmly on his friend's shoulders. There were still no promises, no talk of the title, just of a determination to concentrate on the next match, while Taylor continued to chunter about a need for new players as the Saturdays went by. Of the two games which stand out in the memory of every fan in that era, the first was the 5-0 defeat of Tottenham Hotspur which in some ways provided the pinnacle of the season. Dave Mackay's first opportunity to take on his former teammates was certain to create interest and the crowd of 41,826, a record which was never bettered, were joyously singing 'let them have a kick of the ball' long before the end. Spurs manager Bill Nicholson more or less did my job for me because afterwards I just could not stop him talking:

> They humiliated us. Willie Carlin. What is he? Four foot six? Brilliant. Young McGovern? One minute he's in their penalty area then he's in ours. John O'Hare? You can watch Mike England play for the next five years and you won't see him struggle like that. Dave Mackay? If I wanted all this to happen to anybody it would be him. An inspiration to every-body and a credit to the game.

Clough was what at that time might almost be described as his usual modest self:

> I don't need to say anything, do I? Man of the match? The lads would say John O'Hare and when you see a centre half [Mike England] stumbling around like a blind man I suppose that's fair enough. I think even the idi-ots who don't understand football twigged John O'Hare today.

This was a side-swipe at the fans who regarded O'Hare as too slow. Willie Carlin remembers the game as one of the most enjoyable he ever played – 'we used to play two-touch football in training most days and we beat them by playing two-touch football for ninety minutes. They just couldn't get the ball off us,' he recalled much later. The sign-off line to my Monday match report was a brief one – 'this was not a match, it was a massacre.'

The 4-0 defeat of Liverpool that followed was scarcely less impressive. This was one of the great Liverpool sides, featuring Tommy Smith, Ron Yeats, Ian Callaghan, Roger Hunt, Ian St John and Peter Thompson, Merseyside legends all, but they were run off their feet and poor Yeats suffered the same ordeal as Mike England before him, reduced to cart-horse level by O'Hare's brilliant skills. Bill Shankly had rather less to say than Bill Nicholson, but the message was equally effective. 'To lose 4-0 to that team is no disgrace,' he said, surely one of the greatest compliments any Derby County team has ever been paid. Yet two days later the talk in the manager's office was of other things. Cloughie was adamant he needed to sign a defender, while Peter went further, insisting as he always did that 'two more players and we'll be a team.' Had Peter Taylor been manager of Brazil in 1970 he would have wanted two more players, but where he was right was that the Rams were chronically short of cover in almost every position, which is why they so frequently asked players to turn out when they were far from fully fit.

While it was true that this Derby side was probably much greater than the sum of its parts, it would have required an exceptional player to improve it, something Clough and Taylor recognised, their solution being to sign a very exceptional player indeed and one from just down the road. The target was Terry Hennessey, Nottingham Forest's centre half and at the time without doubt one of the best footballers in Britain. But why would Derby want a centre half when they had Roy McFarland, who was also one of Britain's best, and would Forest be prepared to sell Hennessey anyway? The first question was easily answered, because McFarland was now struggling so badly that he had could hardly train between matches, while Clough also knew Hennessey was a sufficiently versatile and skilful player to take on a midfield role, but as to Forest's willingness to part with their prize asset, well that was something different altogether. The battle for Hennessey went on for around sixteen days, during which the *Derby Telegraph*'s sale was consistently around 108,000 copies a night, an astonishing figure about 12,000 higher than usual, and in the end Clough got his man. Hennessey, Derby's first £100,000 signing, seemed almost as pleased about the deal as Clough and Taylor when I interviewed him at the Baseball Ground the day after he signed and happily agreed to put his name to a piece I would write for him in the following day's *Football Special* without the matter of a fee ever being raised – yet another example of how football and footballers have changed in the last thirty-five years. Perhaps even more surprisingly, when I said I had to catch a bus back into town because my car was off the road, he threw me his keys, told me where his car was, and asked me to drop car and keys back to the Midland Hotel later in the afternoon. I strolled down Shaftsbury Crescent to discover his car – a massive American-style thing – was about twice as long as mine and had a column gear change, something I had never encountered before. It took me about half an hour to manoeuvre it carefully back to work and I was extremely relieved to deliver it to the Midland in one piece as soon as I could. Terry made his debut shortly afterwards against Chelsea, then had a blinder at Burnley – or so I decided from a press box which was so far from the pitch that it was like trying to cover cricket at the County Ground from the top deck of a Nottingham Road bus. Terry Hennessey was a great player and delightful company and it was a shame that Derby did not see the best of him because of the injuries that restricted him to just 79 appearances. A measure of his status was that readers of a TV magazine voted him into a national Great Britain XI, which earned him a trip to Mexico for the 1970 World Cup. Ever on the lookout for ways of earning a few bob, Terry rang to ask whether the *Telegraph* would be interested in some reports from Mexico, an offer I accepted immediately and he duly wrote four excellent long-hand articles which he posted back from South America and were obviously hopelessly out of date by the time they appeared. No laptops or even fax machines in those days. We had agreed a fee of £25 an article and within a couple of days of arriving back in the UK Terry was on the phone – 'Any chance of that hundred quid, George. I'm a bit short?' And I thought footballers were rolling in money.

The Rams' slight falling-off in form as tiredness and injuries took their toll brought further evidence that many supporters had started to take routine brilliance for granted. Certainly the players were starting to look a little jaded, especially those who had played on through no little pain, but that was no excuse for the grumbles and jeers from the terraces and the lady who always sat just behind the press box forever declaring 'too many big dinners in the Midland' when things were not going to her liking. Clough took this in his stride as usual, or at least gave that impression, but he must have felt like throttling some of the Johnny-come-lately critics. He decided to take the players to Guernsey for a few days' relaxation and the change of air obviously helped because two days after their return they beat Arsenal 3-2, Kevin Hector and John O'Hare leading the way. John Roberts was a centre half who relied rather more on brute force than skill and long before the end O'Hare had reduced him to a shambling wreck. It was a good all-round performance and not for the first time I then found it impossible to resist having a pop at the fans, adding that the style of the victory seemed to disappoint some of the crowd who suddenly found they had nothing to complain about. With hindsight it seems the tension was getting to me, supposedly an independent observer, as the season went on.

Terry Hennessey was starting to make a huge difference to the side and played one of his best games for Derby when they won 2-0 at Anfield. It seems remarkable now that a newly promoted side could beat Liverpool 6-0 on aggregate over two games, but that was a measure of the Rams. No wonder Willie Carlin was to say many years later that had Clough and Taylor not left the Baseball Ground Liverpool would have won nothing in the seventies because every cup and title would have finished up at Derby. On that particular day Clough took Bill Shankly by surprise by switching Hennessey to the back four, using Dave Mackay as a sweeper and playing only two men in midfield while Hennessey himself surprised not only Shankly but the entire Kop by thundering into a 50/50 tackle with Tommy Smith that almost landed iron man Smith in Goodison Park. He then scored a brilliant goal, one that was followed by an even more spectacular effort after a thrilling run by Hector and before the end even the loyal Kopites had given it all up as a bad job and started going home. Hector was now back to something like his best and Nottingham Forest doubtless spent the week leading up to the Rams' visit to the City Ground working out how to deal with him, but if they did then it was wasted time, not because Hector was too good for them but because Brian Clough and Peter Taylor were. Shortly before the kick-off it was revealed that Hector would not be playing and that his place would be taken by Frank Wignall, an announcement that prompted confusion and bafflement not only in the press box and the crowd, but also the Forest dressing room, because this was rather like a modern-day cricketer, having spent all week expecting to bat against Shane Warne suddenly discovering it was Brett Lee charging in to bowl at him. Forest manager Matt Gillies, though abrupt and bad mannered in my view, was regarded as a gentleman among football managers because he was quietly spoken and did not throw his weight about, but the team he managed was certainly not created in his public image. Forest were a rough, tough lot and Clough and Taylor obviously thought this was a challenge which might intimidate Hector, but that Wignall would relish. And they were right, as Sammy Chapman, Forest's chief assassin, was soon to discover. Early in the game Wignall ambled towards Chapman as the Forest man launched a long pass downfield and seemed just to brush against him as thousands of pairs of eyes – and certainly those of the referee and linesmen – watched the ball drop towards the Derby penalty area. McFarland headed it back half the length of the pitch and, lo and behold, there was Chapman lying on the floor in obvious agony clutching his ankle. Whatever Wignall did he did very cleverly because afterwards nobody could say precisely how the injury happened, but that was the end of Chapman and Derby won 3-1.

Europe was now surely a racing certainty and all of us looked forward to Easter Monday's home match against Leeds United, but this was to provide a shock of a totally different type. Leeds were due to play Celtic in the European Cup two days later and there was much press speculation about how many players Don Revie would rest so they could be fresh for Europe. As usual we were all in the Midland Hotel on the lunchtime of the game and there was an extra sense of anticipation because rather surprisingly the Leeds party had chosen to dine there as well. I was, as ever, leaning on the bar chatting when Peter Taylor walked in looking unusually serious. 'Would you believe me if I said they've brought the reserves?' he asked in that inimitable corner-of-the-mouth manner, head jerking slightly to one side as he spoke. Peter was always challenging us to believe him, it was one of his favourite expressions, and this time we did because his obvious astonishment said it all. That wonderful, tingling pre-match atmosphere suddenly evaporated. What would the crowd, let alone football officialdom, make of this? Well we soon found out about the crowd, because more than 41,000 were packed into the ground and the reaction when the Leeds team was announced was a predictable barrage of abuse aimed at Don Revie. A comment in my report reflected the mood – 'the crowd was so big the gates were locked 20 minutes before the kick-off… but that was probably to stop them getting out when the teams were announced,' and the fact that Derby's 2-0 win helped their drive for European football was in many respects little consolation. That European place was duly cemented and I could look back with much pleasure on having covered every game in a

Above left: 1 How it all began: Brian Clough signs his first Derby County contract, watched by chairman Sam Longson.

Above right: 2 First mentor: former Derby County manager Harry Storer was Clough's managerial role model. Here Storer talks to Paddy Ryan, who captained the Rams to the Third Division (North) title.

3 Long gone: the seedy but wonderful Cockpit Hill where legendary market trader Mad Harry did his stuff.

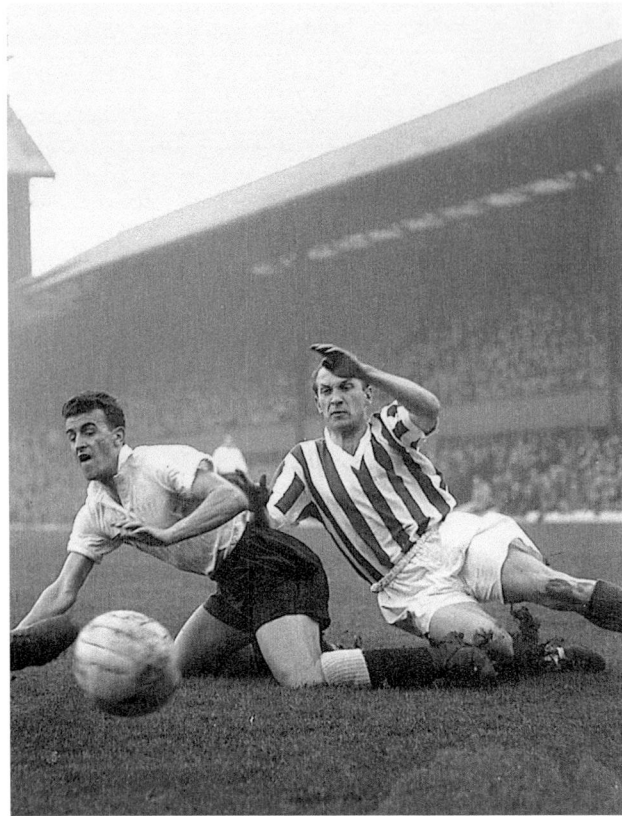

Left: 4 Surely not: a rare picture of Derby County hard man Glyn Davies (left) when he was not clattering into somebody.

Right: 5 Don't mess with me: teammates said that running into Reg Matthews was like tangling with a bag of scrap iron. Matthews was one of England's outstanding goalkeepers during the late 1950s and early '60s.

Opposite above: 6 The goal machine: Brian Clough in action. In his remarkable playing career he averaged almost a goal a game.

Opposite below: 7 Crucial signing: the arrival of Willie Carlin at the Baseball Ground provided the final piece in the Clough and Taylor jigsaw.

Above left: 8 Les Green: short for a goalkeeper but a giant on the pitch. 'For two seasons a match for any goalkeeper in the country,' said Peter Taylor.

Above right: 9 Defensive strongmen: Dave Mackay and Roy McFarland developed a superb partnership, McFarland learning rapidly alongside the Scottish legend.

10 All-time great: Dave Mackay. 'Some people are born with a silver spoon in their mouth. Dave Mackay was born with a silver trophy in his hand,' Brian Clough once said.

Above: 11 Big night: Derby County's Second Division championship celebration dinner at the Pennine Hotel. The author is sitting between Willie Carlin and his wife Marie. Brian Clough is standing on the extreme right.

Right: 12 Camera ready: the always assured Brian Clough gets ready for a lunchtime TV show… with glass in hand.

Above: 13 All well (for the time being): Clough and Taylor sign new contracts at the Baseball Ground watched by Sam Longson and Stuart Webb.

Left: 14 Archie Gemmill: signed for Derby after Brian Clough commandeered his spare bedroom. Gemmill's wife did not care for Brian Clough's TV image but was won over the next morning.

15 Dug-out days: Brian Clough and Peter Taylor prepare for action.

16 Colin Boulton: a fine goalkeeper who would never have moved to Derby but for the recommendation of his pal Nigel Cleevely, who beat him to the Baseball Ground. Despite having to wait a long time for an opportunity, Boulton went on to make 344 first-team appearances.

17 Brave and strong: the great Jackie Stamps, bandaged but unbowed, in action in a cup tie against Queens Park Rangers.

18 Vital goal: John McGovern scores the goal which took Derby County to a crucial home win in the final game of the First Division championship-winning season.

Right: 19 Mud and more mud: how many more goals might Kevin Hector (centre) have scored on today's billiard-table pitches.

Below: 20 My ball: John O'Hare's great skill was on the ground, but here he heads firmly for goal watched by Alan Durban.

21 We'll drink to that: dressing-room champagne after promotion to the First Division is achieved. From left to right: Alan Durban, Roy McFarland, Alan Hinton, Dave Mackay, Kevin Hector, Frank Wignall, Les Green and Ron Webster.

22 Bargain buy: Roger Davies was a huge success after joining Derby County from Southern League Worcester City. His reward for this goal is an embrace from Kevin Hector.

23 Not too bad: Roger Davies was regarded as far stronger on the floor than in the air, but he has no problem winning this ball.

24 A Rams great: Ronnie Webster made 530 first-team appearances for Derby County plus five as a substitute – and it's difficult to remember a poor performance.

25 Simply the best: Roy McFarland and Colin Todd were by some distance the best central-
defensive pairing in the country – quick, skilful and strong.

26 Trophies everywhere.

27 A remarkable record: Geoff Barrowcliffe (left) and Kevin Hector between them made almost 1,100 first-team appearances for Derby County. The delightful Tim Ward, pictured with them, was the man who brought Hector to the Baseball Ground.

28 Not so good: time – and the booze – clearly catching up with Brian Clough towards the end of his days at Forest.

29 Reunion time: the author with Brian Clough at a tribute lunch for the great manager in 2001.

30 Happy days! At the Derby County Former Players Association dinner with John O'Hare, superb centre forward during the club's golden era.

31 Hello again: with Willie Carlin, midfield marvel in Clough and Taylor's promotion side.

32 Brave and composed: Barbara Clough strides proudly from the Pride Park pitch during the Brian Clough Memorial Service after reading a supporter's moving tribute to her late husband.

season which ended with a 12-match unbeaten run and the Rams stunning supporters and sceptics alike by finishing fourth. Taylor, who rarely hung around long after a game ('I'll be shooting off then,' was another favourite of his), stayed for a few beers after the final home game against Wolves, but all was not sweetness and light. There was a real sense of foreboding because the Rams were to be investigated by an FA commission following allegations of financial irregularities. The commission met and a ban from Europe was the inevitable outcome. Clough, who made it fairly clear he thought the whole business was an attempt to get at him because he was unpopular with the football establishment, was furious, but if he felt he was so vulnerable he should have made doubly sure affairs off the field were conducted properly. The fact is they were not and the FA people were simply doing their job. At least Clough and Taylor were young enough to mount another European challenge, something they did with conspicuous success. The disappointed fans also did not have long to wait, but the chance did not come again for one or two and Willie Carlin, who was coming to the end of a distinguished career, long remained justifiably bitter that he had been denied his only chance to play at the highest level in the club game.

CHAPTER 12

FIRST DIVISION CHAMPIONS

The summer flew by. I found any excuse to disappear to the Baseball Ground for hours on end, sometimes just to wander round the pitch with Peter Taylor while he banged on interminably about still needing two new players. These did not arrive for a while, but what Derby County did do was find themselves a new secretary – chief executive these days – a busy, immaculately turned-out young man called Stuart Webb who had been with Preston North End. We were almost the same age and Stuart surprised me by happily revealing his salary, which turned out to be exactly the same as mine. He made a good job of sorting out the behind-the-scenes chaos within the club and I soon concluded there was a lot more money in football than newspapers, for it was not too long before Webby was buying property in Majorca while I was still holidaying in Cromer. He was a good operator and quickly grasped the politics within the club, something which inevitably disconcerted Clough and Taylor, who liked to feel totally in control. The previous secretary, Malcolm Bramley, appointed foolishly on Clough's recommendation at the age of twenty-one, had been out of his depth, but tamely toed the Clough line. Webb was made of stronger stuff and I am not sure whether there was ever a time he and Clough ever entirely trusted the other. Pre-season arrived and I went along to join in a training session at Nottingham Racecourse, where we ran down the finishing straight to a running commentary by Willie Carlin – 'Gleaming Dome leads by half a length from Scouse Git', indicating that he was a yard or two behind prematurely bald Terry Hennessey. The players seemed to have largely come to terms with the disappointment of being denied a place in Europe, but sadly Carlin was soon on his way out of the club in less-than-happy circumstances. The arrival of Archie Gemmill gave Derby a chance to cash in on whatever Willie had left to offer and they sold him to Leicester City, Taylor telling him he was no longer wanted in a brutally short conversation. That was Peter's way – if you decide to do something, get on and do it – but the loyal Carlin, who had contributed so much to the club's success, deserved far better.

Derby had started the season by winning a nondescript pre-season tournament called the Watney Cup, in which they hammered Manchester United 4-0 in the final, a result Clough regarded as the worst thing that could have happened because it would create overconfidence. It possibly did, but the side was soon galvanised by the first of two significant sign-ings, one which has been well documented. Many Rams fans will recall how Clough travelled to Archie Gemmill's Preston home and that when Archie declined to sign straight away, Cloughie refused to budge and fin-ished up staying in the spare room, something which can't have thrilled Mrs Gemmill very much because part of the reason for Archie's hesitancy was that his wife had taken a strong dislike to Clough's television image. But an all-out charm offensive next morning had the required result and Archie signed over breakfast, a decision which made Carlin's departure inevitable. Though he and Carlin were similar in stature, they were very different in style, Gemmill preferring to run with the ball rather than pass it quickly like Willie, but the side eventually adapted and from then on his contribution was a considerable one. The second deal was quite different, involving as it did typical Clough smoke and mirrors. Unlike Gemmill, who was something of an unknown, Colin Todd was regarded as one of the best young players in the country and there was some sur-prise when Sunderland announced he was for sale, an announcement followed quickly by bluff and counter-bluff among the big clubs as they all denied any interest in signing Todd while at the same time working away to do exactly that. 'Not for us. He's just a bread and butter player and in any case he's far too expensive,' said Clough before getting into his car and setting of, to Sunderland to get the deal under way. I knew noth-ing of this until Brian's early-morning call the next day – 'If you'd like to meet Colin Todd get yourself down here as soon as you can.'

Clough and Taylor were now well on the way to creating their second great Derby County side, though a final position of ninth in the table was the best they could manage. It was a stop-start season, one stop being an unscheduled one on the way back from a night game at Coventry when I suffered a recurrence of my schoolboy travel sickness and had to ask for the coach to be pulled over for a few minutes so I could get off and walk up and down in the fresh air. My walk lasted about sixty seconds before I was violently ill all over the grass verge, prompting a cheer and a round of applause on the bus. Thankfully there were several far more savoury moments on the pitch, notably a brilliant 4-1 win at West Ham where Alan Hinton scored one of the most remarkable goals I have ever seen. Having already scored a blinder with his left foot, Hinton this time used his right to devastating effect. Faced by a retreating wall of West Ham defenders, Hinton looked up to see goalkeeper Peter Grotier just off his line and, from about twenty yards out, suddenly stabbed down on the ball, sending it soaring into the air where it hung, spinning viciously, before dropping behind Grotier and just under the crossbar. I described it at the time as being like a golfer holing in one on a par-four hole, but actually it was the equivalent of chipping straight in from a bunker fifty yards from the green. As the ball dropped almost vertically into the net, Hinton watched with the rest of us, then fell backwards and executed a perfect Dave Mackay backward somersault. That season, of course, saw the departure of the great Mackay who was true to himself to the very end. In the final game of the season against West Bromwich Albion at the Baseball Ground, Dave was still rushing to take a throw-in with two minutes to go even though Derby were 2-0 ahead and still clapping urgently until the final whistle, upon which he raced off with just the briefest wave to the crowd. What a man and what a shame he could not have been around for just one more season.

Again the summer seemed over in a flash and we were off, every-body in high spirits and confident, supporters too, a confidence which showed early signs of being justified. It was not until the thirteenth game that Derby were beaten, yet Clough was dismissive of title talk, as were much of the southern press who did not seem overly fond of Cloughie, nor this team which was spoiling the party attended normally only by London, Manchester and Liverpool. Win followed win, Derby often driving teams to distraction by the way in which they retained posses-sion, creating frustration which boiled over from time to time and led to the odd comic moment. At Everton little Jimmy Husband lost his com-posure completely when Archie Gemmill bamboozled him and chased

Archie for about twenty yards before bringing him down from behind. Unfortunately he injured himself in the process and was booked by the referee while lying flat on his back receiving treatment. Derby players were so much in control at that time that they rarely fell foul of referees though Kevin Hector managed to get himself booked without fouling anybody, speaking to anybody or showing the slightest sign of emotion, quite an unusual achievement. Racing from just inside the Derby half, he had run on to a pass and was hurtling towards goal completely clear when the linesman's flag belatedly went up for offside. Kevin picked up the ball, ran back past the referee without giving him a glance, and carefully placed it about a foot inside his own half, clearly indicating that he knew where he had been when the ball was played. The crowd erupted with laughter, but the ref did not see the funny side of it and Kevin went into his book.

Work was non-stop pleasure and match days a joy – one in particular, for reasons which had little to do with football. It was years since I had seen George Brown, still MP for Belper and by then, I think, Foreign Secretary, so it was a nice surprise to see him sitting at the bar of the Midland Hotel, gin and tonic in hand, when I arrived at the Midland Hotel before a game against West Ham United. I had invited my father along to the game and as we approached George, he slid from his stool, thrust out his hand and uttered the warmest welcome. I thrust my hand out too, only to be ignored completely as George embarked on a lengthy and vigorous handshake with my startled father, insisting he had a drink and demanding to know how he was and what he had been up to. This would have been tricky enough had my father known who it was offering this generous hospitality, but as somebody with not the slightest interest in politics, he had absolutely no idea who he was talking to. 'I didn't realise you two were friends,' I whispered while Brown ordered drinks. 'We're not. Who is he?' replied my father who was totally taken aback when I told him he was talking to one of the most important men in the land. Things improved when I managed to infiltrate the conversation and remind George of my days as a young reporter in Belper, which thankfully he remembered. Knowing him to be a keen West Ham supporter I assumed he was going to the match, but he explained that much as he would like to, he had an important meeting with some German businessmen in London and was catching the 12.30 train. Twenty minutes and another gin and tonic later I pointed to my watch, but George airily waved me away, insisting there was no problem because he could catch the 1.30 and still make the meeting in plenty of time. We chatted away happily about football, politics and Belper, George drinking gin after gin until, around 1.20, I again reminded him of the time and again my concerns were dismissed, because apparently even the 2.30 train would enable him to keep his appointment. Half an hour or so later my father and I made our farewells and headed off to the Baseball Ground and soon all thoughts of George Brown, trains and Germans were forgotten. Half-time came and I shot down from the press box to the gents' toilets, from which was coming the lustiest rendition of 'I'm Forever Blowing Bubbles' I had heard for years. Immediately knowing what to expect, I pushed the door open to find George Brown in full voice while dispatching a fair proportion of his liquid lunch. He glanced round and, seeing my look of horror, said, 'Don't worry. If I get the 5.30 I can take them for dinner.' Whether he made the 5.30, or indeed any other train that evening, I never discovered.

Derby was a hubbub of football talk. It seemed nothing else mattered, though those affected by the crash of Rolls-Royce might not have seen it like that. Leeds United and Manchester City were leading the way, but Derby were closing all the time and as City faltered in the home straight, the Rams went to the top of the table with a 4-0 romp away to Sheffield United, having a week earlier given Clough immense pleasure by comprehensively beating Leeds United. In a sense it was a dream-like sensation for those close to the club; I am not sure we could quite comprehend what was happening and Clough finally stopped insisting that his team were not good enough to become champions. There was a major hiccup when they lost 2-0 at Maine Road, where Rodney Marsh beat them almost single-handedly, but they rounded off the season with a magnificent 1-0 win over Liverpool at the Baseball Ground. This match has been well chronicled, though not by me. I had been feeling rough for a couple of days and about half an hour into the game was overcome by nausea and had to ask Gerald Mortimer to report the game as I just had to get out of the ground. I wandered up and down outside for twenty minutes or so before deciding to call it a day and as I trudged slowly back into town heard a colossal roar which told me Derby had scored. It was all a bit embarrassing and Peter Taylor told me next day he thought it was all down to nerves and there was nothing wrong with me at all. I protested vigorously, but I cannot say for certain that he was entirely wrong. Fortunately I had been there long enough to see sixteen-year-old Steve Powell, on his first full appearance, make a complete mug of Emlyn Hughes, flicking the ball over the England star's head and coolly regathering it with a nonchalance of which George Best would have been proud. Even after this crucial victory the tension was not over, indeed it was increasing, because though Derby were top they had completed their fixtures, while the pursuing Leeds and Liverpool each had a game in hand and could still overtake them. The odds were surely on one of these sides winning, but Liverpool were held to a goalless draw at Arsenal and Wolves somehow beat Leeds 2-1, leaving the Rams clear by a single point. Some sections of the London press remained churlish, suggesting that Derby had won the title by default, a bizarre accusation given that they accumulated more points than the other clubs over a small matter of 42 games, which is the way titles tend to be won. Bill Shankly was more generous, describing the Rams as not only the best team in the country but also the most entertaining, and assuming Shanks was right, then what made that especially remarkable was that the Baseball Ground pitch was a quagmire for half the season. Some described it as like playing on a ploughed field, but there was so much sand on it that it was more like playing on Skegness beach just after the tide had gone out. What sort of brilliance they might have produced on today's billiard-table surfaces can only be imagined. The celebration dinner which followed was a curious affair, attended by a large number of guests invited by the council, some of whom apparently had little idea what the function was all about, but were there because they were considered to be important. I made my own mark on the occasion by hiring a dinner suit which was far too small and, since I could not find any black socks, wearing a grey woolly pair, much to the amusement of my colleagues on the press table. A flat cap and I could probably have done a passable Norman Wisdom impression

EVERYBODY WANTS TO beat the champions and several did as the Rams started the following season catastrophically, struggling along for weeks towards the foot of the table. There were some great results and some terrible ones and I am struck looking back at our match reports how remarkably unbiased we were. When things went wrong neither Gerald Mortimer nor I seemed to have any fear of getting stuck into players and management and we were frequently unimpressed by the quality of refereeing, too, Gerald memorably describing one incompetent as 'referereeing in a blithe cocoon of self-congratulation', a description I would have rather liked to have thought up. Clough and Taylor were hugely irritated by the team's inconsistency, though it was in part created by a spate of injuries. The European Cup, as it was then called, brought out the best in the players, however. They beat Zeljeznicar Sarajevo 4-1 on aggregate, a tie Peter Taylor was relieved to see the back of in part because it meant he no longer had to grapple hopelessly and hilariously with trying to pronounce their name. They then produced a series of worryingly modest League performances as they prepared for two games against Benfica, opposition of an altogether different quality. They played so poorly in their final match before the first leg at the Baseball Ground that the national press wrote off their chances completely – 'Easy Prey for the Eagles' was one headline – but on the night the Rams produced thirty minutes of the most remarkable football ever seen at the ground and that was all it needed. Roy McFarland scored early on with a superb header, Kevin Hector added a second and when John McGovern curled in a magnificent third just before the half-hour the game was over. The great Eusebio, scarcely given a sniff by McFarland, walked off at the end looking stunned and neither was he given much of a look-in two weeks later when the sides drew 0-0, though it took a couple of magnificent saves by Colin Boulton to deny him as a roaring 75,000 crowd in Lisbon was reduced to silence.

This triumph kick-started the season, but by now all I was getting on my visits to the Baseball Ground were long laments from Brian and Peter about the way the club was disintegrating off the field. Their feud with the directors was becoming more unpleasant by the day and I had a go at all and sundry in the paper, accusing both management and directors of allowing politics and childish vendettas to put the club's success in jeopardy. Neither Clough nor Taylor even mentioned the piece, for that was how they were, but Sam Longson, who had regained the chairmanship, was beside himself with rage and as a result we had a stand-up row in the press room before the next game, Longson waving the paper in my face and shouting while I told him that I could write what I liked so long as it was not libellous. There was some clearing of the air, but not much and Longson and I largely stayed clear of one another after that. Six weeks or so later, when the Rams headed off to London for an FA Cup replay against Spurs, I travelled down by train with Albert Mays, the former

Rams player, who was running the office local. I suppose I realised, as Albert struggled to carry his suitcase, gasping for breath and stopping for a rest every fifty yards or so, that he was seriously ill and sadly it turned out to be the last game he ever saw. Neither of us was to know that, of course, as we watched yet another of those occasional displays of stupendous brilliance that made this era so memorable. Despite dominating the game completely the Rams were 3-1 down with only twelve minutes to go and apparently on their way out when Roger Davies, enjoying the game of his life, stunned White Hart Lane by scoring twice to make it 3-3 and almost snatching a winner as Derby stormed the home goal. When the whistle went at the end of normal time, the Spurs management team dashed on to the field and started issuing instructions for all they were worth, while Clough and Taylor sat arms folded in the dugout, not even bothering to move. It was another masterstroke, indicating that so far as they were concerned the game was up for Tottenham and so it proved. Derby devoted extra time to a blissful display of exhibition football during which they scored twice, could have had four or five more, and finished up so much on top that when the whistle went the entire crowd of almost 53,000 stood and applauded them from the field. Terry Venables, whose QPR team were next up for the Rams, wandered past shortly afterwards, glanced across grinning broadly, shrugged his shoulders and just said 'What a team'. It was indeed magnificent and I was not alone in wondering out loud whether any club side in the world could beat them in that form

Derby did not, of course, always play to such a level because no team could and they could certainly not legislate for the vagaries of refereeing and the dark side of the game. Their biggest challenge of the season came when they travelled to Turin to play Juventus in the semi-final of the European Cup, where a curious chain of events unfolded. First Archie Gemmill had his name taken for an innocuous half-challenge, then Roy McFarland was booked simply for heading away a free-kick under pressure from a Juventus attacker. By a remarkable coincidence – or not – these were the two players who had been cautioned previously in the tournament which meant they would miss the second leg, which was all very convenient from a Juventus point of view. Clough and Taylor were seething, Taylor complaining bitterly that referee and linesmen had been given designer wristwatches worth around £3,000 each before the game as a 'memento' of the occasion (Derby traditionally gave small pieces of Crown Derby), but I suspect there was far more to it than that. The *Sunday Times* spent years investigating allegations of bribery, but did not really get anywhere. If it is hard to root out corruption in the English game, what chance in Italy?

So that was the end of Derby County in Europe and it was almost the end of Derby County for me, too. At the start of the season I had stood in the press box running through the fixtures, when it dawned on me in a curiously depressing kind of way that I already knew where I was going to be every Saturday for the next eight or nine months and rather than feeling excited I had more a sense of 'here we go again'. Was I going to do this for the next thirty years? Some time later, while travelling back from a dinner at Uttoxeter Racecourse with the *Telegraph*'s editor John Low, I casually mentioned that if the opportunity ever arose I would not mind returning to general news, a remark that so shocked John I though he might crash the car. He, like others at the paper I suppose, thought I had the most exciting job in the building and was amazed I was prepared to give it up, but I was and when, later in the season, he told me our assistant editor Bob Randall was taking over as editor at Stoke-on-Trent and I was welcome to take his place, I decided I would.

CHAPTER 13

FAREWELL BRIAN AND LIFE AFTER SPORT

And so after thirteen years of non-stop sport, most of it spent out of the office and all of it great fun, I suddenly found myself in charge of the paper whenever the editor was away, a slightly unreal sensation given that Norman Peace, who had been news editor when I joined the paper as a sixteen-year-old trainee, was still running the news desk in his grumpy but efficient style. Norman, by then close to retirement, was a decent old stick and popular with reporters and if he felt awkward about some-body half his age chasing him up, he certainly did not let on. For the most part, in any case, I was kept busy checking page proofs to ensure stories and headlines were up to scratch, which seemed fairly tedious after the excitement of life at the Baseball Ground. Not long afterwards, however, I was back in the thick of it again. Though trying hard not to tread on Gerald Mortimer's toes, for he had succeeded me as sports editor as well as full-time Derby County reporter, I still saw a good deal of Brian Clough because we had become close friends and it was clear from everything he told me that his relationship with the Derby County directors was deteriorating ever more rapidly. Gerald obviously saw this, too, and feared – as I did – that Brian and Peter Taylor would leave. They had not been short of offers previously, notably from Coventry City, Birmingham City and even Barcelona and from time to time, whether through conceit or simple overconfidence, had made it very obvious that so far as they were concerned they had complete control and would walk away if their authority was reduced or even threatened. What they did not do was take note that Jack Kirkland had joined the board of directors. I never got to know Kirkland very well, perhaps because I had taken a dislike to him from the moment we were introduced, but he had obviously taken it upon himself to put Clough and Taylor in their place, which might have been acceptable given some of their excesses, but for the manner in which he went about it. What motivated him is hard to fathom, because no normal person would want to be remembered only for driving Derby County's most successful ever managerial team out of the club, but he tackled the job with relish, getting at Clough through the more vulnerable Taylor. He started to challenge Peter at every opportunity, forever wanting to know where he had been and why, which was extraordinary in view of everything he had achieved. Peter was evidently getting more and more depressed by this hounding and this in turn was making Brian angrier by the day, because while he knew deep down that they took liberties, so far as he was concerned their success entitled them to operate in the way that had so far worked so well. However, by now Kirkland was also making bullets for Sam Longson to fire directly at the manager – the same Longson, of course, who had stood at the front of the Highbury directors' box on the night Derby had clinched the First Division title, waving grandly to the crowd as if he had just become emperor of Rome. So far as he was concerned he was the driving force and therefore deserved the credit, a ludicrous self-deception which Kirkland did nothing to discourage.

Unfortunately Brian had not helped himself by some of his outrageous comments on television and in his newspaper column. Some may well have been justified, like his lambasting of the FA over its tolerant attitude towards Leeds United's misdemeanours, but when he accused FA members of having a vested interest and not treating all clubs the same, he was on very thin ice indeed and playing into the directors' hands by risking a charge of bringing the game into disrepute. There is no question, either, that his early and very likeable forthright self-confidence had to some extent evolved into a bumptious arrogance which could sometimes embarrass his closest friends, not least Taylor. In this respect he was not helped by his one real ally on the board, Mike Keeling, who had not only apparently appointed himself Brian's personal slave, but in some ways more damagingly was forever telling him what he wanted to hear. It was difficult to dislike Keeling, but he became acolyte rather than advisor, so much so that he even adopted the Clough nasal drawl and picked up many of his mannerisms. I suspect that if Mike had been firm with Clough and told him to calm down, become less confrontational and just dig his heels in, Brian would probably have done so and the entire outcome might have been different. Gerald Mortimer, though in a difficult position since he was theoretically detached from the politics of the club, certainly tried to dissuade Brian and Peter from resigning and I don't blame him. There are times when professional considerations can reasonably be set aside and I would have done the same had it been me sitting with them at the ground. But by now it was too late, because though they did not recognise it at the time they had been completely outflanked by Longson and Kirkland, who had enticed them into the resignation trap. Sometime after lunch on 15 October I had a telephone call from Brian with the request I had expected but dreaded and so telephoned the sports editor of the *Daily Mail* in London to see how much they would pay for Cloughie's exclusive account of his resignation. The answer to this question was, if I remember rightly, £1,500 and so Jeff Farmer, then the *Mail*'s man in the Midlands, got his story, later thanking me at length over a few beers in the York Hotel. A few days later I received a cheque from the *Mail* for £15, along with a letter of thanks suggesting I treat my family to a slap-up meal. Those were the days.

As any Derby County fan will know there was pandemonium over the next few days as fans and players reacted furiously. I did my best to keep out of it, because it was now Gerald Mortimer's show, but players rang from time to time either wanting information or urging the paper to mount a campaign to have the management team reinstated, something which was impossible because Brian and Peter had not been sacked, they had left of their own accord. I saw little of Taylor at this time, Peter having recognised immediately that it was all over and indicated he was ready to move on. His health was not especially good and in any case he had accepted there could never be a reconciliation with Longson and Kirkland, which was a rather more realistic position than Cloughie took. Brian was orchestrating player rebellion for all he was worth and moaned to me quite a bit about the paper not backing him sufficiently, conveniently forgetting that it was he who had taken the decision to resign and he who had been completely outmanoeuvred. We did not fall out about it and so far as I know he did not fall out with Gerald either, but there were a few difficult conversations before things settled down again. When Nottingham Forest were becoming a power in Europe only half a dozen years later there must have been many a frustrated Derby

County fan wondering what might have happened had Clough and Taylor reacted differently to the provocation, found a compromise and remained at the Baseball Ground. Willie Carlin, of course, had always insisted that had that been the case Liverpool would have won nothing in the 1970s and who is to say he was wrong? They left a superb team at the Baseball Ground, with the squad significantly strengthened not long before they resigned by the signing of David Nish. One of Clough's most significant comments when he finally admitted defeat and settled for temporary obscurity was one he made to supporters at a public meeting organised by the hastily formed Derby County Protest Movement held at the King's Hall. 'If you watch football for another forty years I don't think you will ever see more character, more intelligence and more talent on one field,' he said. Character and talent we knew about and under-stood, but his choice of the word intelligence was instructive. Clough was not, of course, suggesting his players could have romped unbeaten through a season of *University Challenge*, but emphasising that a player with intelligence to go with his talent and character was always likely to be more successful then one who relied entirely on natural gifts and a good work ethic. So how would the team have developed had he stayed? Appreciative though he was of the contribution of John Robson, a left-back who was naturally right-footed, Clough and Taylor were desperate to sign Mike Pejic, the Stoke City left-back, whose defensive qualities and uncomplicated attacking skills they much admired. The back four they secretly hoped to create would have read Nish, Todd, McFarland and Pejic – 'with those four you would stand back at the start of the season and challenge any side to score a goal against you,' said Clough. Derby rather than Forest would have made the first £1 million signing because Trevor Francis would have been signed, so would Gary Birtles and those two would quite probably have been joined by Tommy Hutchinson, the Coventry City outside left, when the time came to replace Alan Hinton. Taylor was particularly keen to sign Hutchinson, a direct, skilful, quick and brave winger who could go past people at the sort of pace that will always unsettle defences. Peter even devised a plan to surprise opposi-tion sides in the course of certain matches by switching him to centre forward – 'he causes chaos out wide, so imagine him running at defences through the middle,' he said, but whether he was right about this we were never to discover, because so far as Derby County were concerned Clough and Taylor were now officially part of their history.

I was soon thinking about other things, not least how I was going to stay sane now I was neither writing nor getting out and about meeting people. The decision to abandon sports writing was not something I did on impulse, but I soon realised I missed it and at one point was very tempted to accept Frank Nicklin's offer to join *The Sun*. Frank, once a Derby sports writer himself and a very popular Fleet Street sports editor, did not exactly headhunt me, far from it. He simply said I could have a job if I wanted one and as I could not make my mind up either way I did what I have always tended to do and took the safe option and stayed where I was. But I felt I had to write something, so started reviewing shows at the grandly named Talk of the Midlands in Mill Street. The Talk, as it was known to all, has long gone, but for a time it attracted not just major British stars but big names from America and Europe, the only drawback for me being that the top-of-the-bill act often did not come on stage until after midnight, which meant a very late night and a fairly regular Monday-morning headache. The club was owned and run by Julian Beck and one of Derby's most colourful characters Tommy Barnes, an irresistible personality and a very good friend. Tommy had a gravy-stained tie for every occasion, a broad grin, a remarkably quick wit and an equally remarkable capacity for polishing off huge amounts of whisky. He was a larger-than-life entertainer who drew people to him, so much so that some landlords were happy for him to drink for next to nothing because he attracted other customers. 'A large Scotch and 10p in the swear box,' he would announce on his arrival at the bar, then keep us all amused until he moved on to some other watering hole. Entertainers who came to the Talk of the Midlands thought the world of him, especially Les Dawson, who always said he enjoyed coming to Derby because he would go away at the end of the week with a couple of Barnes one-liners he could use in his act. It was Tommy who years before had opened Uncle Tom's Cabin, the tea bar next to the Market Hall, and he frequently turned up there with people like Gene Pitney and Frankie Vaughan (or Frank Vaughan as he much preferred to be called), who would happily sit with a mug of tea alongside shoppers and market traders. Pitney had no pretensions and was good company, though if the subject ever turned to do-it-yourself or home improvements he could bore for Britain, or Tulsa perhaps. Frank Vaughan was a regular visitor and inevitably celebrated his birthday in Derby, grinning that cheesy Vaughan grin for the *Telegraph* photographer as he cut a cake provided by fans. It was probably at least three years before I realised that Frank did not always come to Derby in the same month let alone the same week, so I assume he had at least fifty-two birthdays a year, one for each venue.

Without doubt the nicest showbusiness person to appear at the Talk was Ruby Murray, whose name will live on if only in rhyming slang legend. Ruby spoke as she sang and her lovely soft Irish accent and easy smile had the men round the bar weak at the knees, no knees weaker than mine. Sadly her career had long been in decline by the time she started visiting Derby and it was by the bar she was usually to be found. She had a reputation for drinking heavily and alcohol was certainly regarded as a major cause of her early death, but I thought she was wonderful and if she had drunk more than she should she never showed it. The same could not be said for Tommy Cooper, who had frequently drunk more than he should when he was in Derby and always showed it. Cooper was one of those 'like them or loath them' comics and I was firmly in the camp which thought he was one of the funniest men who ever set foot on a stage, though this rebounded on me on one occasion. I made the mistake of writing that Tommy could be funny without actually doing anything – something with which most of his fans would agree – but he misunderstood this completely, taking my comment to mean that he did not do anything funny. I was not aware of this and turned up again the night the review appeared looking forward to watching him again. I was standing in the green room next to the stage when the compère Pete Conway came on and did the introduction, inevitably ending with the usual 'so will you welcome, please, the one and only Mr Tommy Cooper.' There was huge applause, but when the curtains opened nobody was to be seen. We were all wondering when he was going to appear when from behind one curtain at the side of the stage came a booming voice. 'Is George Edwards in?' Then after a further poise, 'Is he in? If he is, tell him I'm coming out to do nothing.' Those who knew me turned to see my reaction and I had, I'm sure, gone bright scarlet. I did not have the faintest idea what he was talking about, but Tommy Barnes soon came bustling over to tell me that Cooper had been complaining ever since he arrived at the club that night and wanted to see me afterwards to demand an apology. I felt I had to stay around, feeling distinctly nervous, and sure enough when the show ended in he came and Barnes introduced us. Cooper, a huge man who towered over me, did not shake hands, but just stared at me for a few seconds, which was absolutely the worst thing he could have done. I started giggling, so did the people who were watching all this and, thankfully, so did he until everybody was laughing like idiots. When we had all calmed down he went off to the bar and returned with a large glass of red wine. 'You probably think I'm drinking this,' he said, 'but actually I'm doing nothing.' If I remember rightly he did not turn up at all a couple of nights later because he was too drunk to leave his hotel, but that was the way he lived his life.

Though this was a one-off confrontation, I never ceased to be surprised by how seriously these well-established entertainers took a six- or seven-paragraph review in a relatively small provincial newspaper. Having once written that the Barron Knights, the comedy band, should sing more straight numbers because their talent as musicians was overshadowed by their emphasis on humour, I was approached by their leader, a little fellow with a mass of curly fair hair, who wanted to discuss how they could improve their act. And he was perfectly serious.

Of course not all those who appeared at the Talk were big names. Some hopefuls never made the grade at all, while others went on to much greater things having cut their teeth in the clubs. Dustin Gee, a young comedian who was both funny and clever, was at the foot of the bill when he first appeared and therefore first on when the place was barely half full. He was quite touchingly thrilled when I wrote that he would soon be back topping the bill, but less than a year later he was doing just that and was so obviously talented that he teamed up with Les Dennis for a very successful television series. Dustin could have gone on and made a big name for himself in a Larry Grayson sort of way, but his health was never very good and he died from heart trouble while still a relatively young man. Peter Conway, a regular compère at the Talk, was a top-rate club singer-comedian who later spent a lot of time working in big holiday centres and many years after the Tommy Cooper incident, while on a family holiday, we spotted his name outside a holiday park in South Wales and decided to go in and seek him out. Peter was found and we had chatted about old times for half an hour or so when a boy of about fourteen or fifteen appeared and stood head down while his father introduced him as his son Rob. 'Pleased to meet you, Rob,' I said, before asking rather patronisingly whether he would like to follow his father into showbusiness when he was older. Still staring at the floor he nodded and muttered that he would and, shy lad though he obviously was back then, he did just that and made rather a success of it, too – under the name of Robbie Williams rather than Rob Conway.

Most of the Talk's star names stayed at the York Hotel, but not always. There was a Saturday when I was particularly keen to see an England rugby international on television and asked Bill Wainwright, then manager of the Midland Hotel, whether I might watch it in the television room there, something he was happy for me to do though he would not be around himself as he was going on holiday. When I arrived on the Saturday I sought out the relief manager, told him I had spoken to Mr Wainwright and was ushered upstairs to a private room where I found the television already on, a bottle of whisky and a plate of sandwiches, 'and do give us a call if there is anything else you need,' he said before disappearing downstairs. I tucked into the sandwiches and the Scotch thinking Bill had done me rather proud and was looking forward to the match when the relief manager reappeared and asked, 'do you have any idea exactly what time Miss Bassey will be arriving?' Disconcerted to say the least I muttered something about not being quite certain then as soon as he had left the room beat a hasty retreat and watched the rugby in the Merry Widows pub across the road. I assume Shirley Bassey and her entourage sorted out more sandwiches when they arrived.

The impressionist Mike Yarwood, who also stayed at the Midland Hotel, had just included Brian Clough in his repertoire when he came to Derby, so he went down wonderfully well, especially with Brian who went along to watch. Afterwards we all went back to the Midland where Cloughie must have told Yarwood at least twenty times, 'Hey, you're right at the top of your profession, just like me,' which Yarwood's manager found highly amusing. Brian went home at some point but the rest of us stayed talking until I suddenly realised it was nearly light and that I might as well have a couple of cups of coffee and go straight to work. Plenty of stamina in those days. The glam-rock band Slade were good value, too. They were looking for somewhere to go after doing an interview on Radio Derby, so I suggested the Grandstand Hotel at the County Ground where the landlord Charles Townsend had little regard for licensing hours. Townsend welcomed us all then disappeared, leaving us to run the bar, which was very trusting of him. Noddy Holder liked a cigar and had at least three, making sure he paid at least the right money if not more. They were nice lads just loving what they were doing; not a big head among them. When we left I closed the door behind us then realised I had left my new sheepskin coat inside. I was very proud of this coat because the (then) young commentator John Motson had made them rather fashionable, but I reckoned that as the pub was now shut it would still be there if I called back dead on opening time. This I did to discover a police car outside. There had been a break-in and thieves had stolen money, cigarettes… and the sheepskin coat I had left lying on the back of a chair.

Tommy Barnes brought a lot to Derby because there was no other live entertainment apart from the Playhouse, but he and Julian Beck were eventually brought down by the greed of the business. Acts which had demanded perhaps £1,200 a week suddenly started asking £1,700 and there was no way Barnes and Beck could pay that sort of money. Their answer was to go for smaller, lesser-known artists, but the public did not want to know and before long the Talk closed after a big last-night party at which some staff, having not been paid, grabbed anything they could and carted it off. It was an unhappy end. Barnes went back to market trading, something he did with panache alongside his cousin Jack ('Applejack') Woodhouse. He was, however, broke and with creditors closing in from all directions, filed for bankruptcy. Down though he was and unusually depressed, Tommy Barnes could never be anything other than himself. The receiver was not impressed by what he was told at the hearing and rounded off a long lecture by glaring severely at Tom and saying, 'and so, Mr Barnes, you have earned thousands of pounds and you have spent thousands of pounds, much of it on alcohol and what do you have to show for it?' Tommy stared straight back: 'Sclerosis of the liver, sir,' he replied with a bright smile. Tom Barnes was wrong about that, but he was certainly not well. He had piled weight on and was drinking more than ever so it was no real surprise when very early one morning one of his close pals Derek Thorpe rang to tell me Tommy had suffered a massive heart attack and died within minutes. His funeral was a huge affair attended by hundreds including many from showbusiness, who spoke fondly of him at the party which followed at the York Hotel. Tom was a little too rough and ready for some tastes and was almost certainly a little wayward with his tax and VAT returns but he was a wonderful character and so, in her way, was Alice Baker, the legendary large and ancient landlady of the White Horse Hotel who sat every day holding court in the Virgin's Corner, a tiny bar at the back of the pub, from which she moved only occasionally and then very slowly, head bobbing from side to side like a giant tortoise in search of something to eat. In Alice's case she was usually on the lookout for somebody to buy her a drink or perhaps for a young couple to admonish for holding hands. Alice did not approve of physical contact in her pub and neither was it a good idea to buy her a drink for this would usually prompt her to announce that George (or whoever) was buying drinks if anybody would like one. Alice insisted that when she died the funeral cortège should drive past every pub she had kept in the town on its way to the crematorium. When the day came this request made it a long journey and if she was cremated wearing all her jewellery it would have required six Olympic weightlifters to carry her coffin into the crematorium.

Not all Derby's characters were lovable eccentrics. The Exchange Hotel, next door to the former *Telegraph* office, was the haunt of many local criminals, something which suited the police because it meant they usually knew where to find them. Most were small-time thieves who were always in and out of court but never caused any problems for the landlord Jack Beckett and his formidable wife Rose, who came from a tough fairground family and took no nonsense. Market traders, journalists, local businessmen and these petty rogues coexisted perfectly peaceably in what was a fairly typical city-centre pub, but when I called in late one evening I was surprised to see a rather different calibre of criminal sitting at the end of the bar. I had known Albert Jones fairly well for a few years. He was the youngest of the Jones family who had developed quite a reputation during the Teddy Boy era of the 1950s. Georgie Jones, the oldest brother, had mellowed into a nice old boy, still wearing his velvet-collar suit and big-soled suede shoes thirty years after Elvis Presley had arrived on the scene, but Albert, the youngest, was dangerous because he was completely unpredictable. He was no more than five feet nine inches tall if that and probably weighed about eleven stone, but he was all bone and muscle and many a time had taken on two or three men and laid them all out. I was hardly pleased to see him, but Albert was on his own that night so when he waved an obvious wave of welcome I went across to talk to him rather than risk causing offence. We talked about boxing, which was all we had in common, and I raised the subject of Dave 'Boy' Green, one of the big names of the day who was not much of a boxer but had a whirlwind style that brought him many victories and excited the public. I ventured to say that Green was a crowd pleaser, 'and it's nice to see a real fighter for a change.'

'He's not a fighter,' said Albert quietly, prompting me to make the foolishly dangerous mistake of insisting Green must be a fighter because he did not box, just threw punches. 'He's not a fighter,' Albert repeated firmly and I quickly realised that not only had his voice changed but his eyes as well. 'No, you're right,' I replied, finishing my drink as quickly as I could and making for the door, claiming I had to pop back into the office. A narrow escape perhaps. The next morning I was in work early and went to see the news editor Chris Ward to find out what was going on.

'We've got a murder,' said Chris. 'And it's a good one. Albert Jones.'

I was stunned. 'Good grief, I was with him last night. Who has he killed?'

'He's not killed anybody,' said Chris. 'It's Albert who's been murdered.'

It emerged that soon after I left the pub Albert Jones had headed home to be confronted by a man with a carving knife who, I think, had some grudge to settle over a debt. Jones was unarmed and his attacker stabbed him several times but, said the police, he would not go down and kept coming back at his attacker until he finally fell to the floor. He was later shown to be covered in scars, evidence of previous battles including one famous encounter in Leicester Prison when he was challenged by the prison hard man who knew of his reputation and wanted to establish who was kingpin. From all accounts Albert made mincemeat of him. A very frightening man.

Life meandered on. The *Evening Telegraph* moved from its city-centre offices to a new building near the railway station so the office pub was now the Cattle Market – later the Smithfield – which was the haunt of many of the older market traders, some of whom had maintained the pre-freezer tradition of swapping perishable goods between themselves at the end of the week rather than throwing them away. I occasionally got involved in this when somebody would show me a business letter that needed a formal reply. I would provide this, in return for which I might get a lump of cheese or some lamb chops. A poulterer once said he had a chicken for me, but when I discovered it was running around squawking in the back of his van decided to have a pint by way of payment instead. Not that I was spending much time in the pub. I was now nearing forty and training hard because my next birthday meant I could compete in veteran races. I kept work clothes at the office and ran to and from work most days – a circuitous ten-mile route each way on a Monday and

Thursday, shorter runs the other days plus sixteen to twenty miles on a Sunday. Thus my first company car did little more than 1,500 miles in its first twelve months and I got fit enough to pick up a few prizes. But where was my career going? Traditionally Northcliffe Newspapers never promoted from within at management level so I knew I had to move to get on and early in 1983 that opportunity came with a chance to move to Wales. I travelled to Swansea by train to have a look at the place and, like so many before me, was horrified as we travelled through the industrial ugliness of Port Talbot and the eastside of Swansea. This was not the Peak District. I stayed in the city's famous Dragon Hotel and, first thing in the morning, put my kit on and ran down the seafront to Mumbles and back, an easy – and flat – run of about ten miles that changed my perception completely. The tide was in, the sun was out and I was hooked so I accepted the job without another thought. For all that, the drive down to Swansea with my family after an epic farewell party was a journey of mixed emotions. We were moving away from the only place we had known and leaving behind a host of friends, among them one of the greatest football managers of all time, perhaps the greatest.

CHAPTER 14

THE BOYS DONE WELL

Midway through the 1960s, just before I became sports editor I was joined on the *Derby Telegraph* sports desk by a bright young lad from the north-east called Vic Wakeling, pleasant, talented, but hard-nosed and obviously ambitious and Vic and I, along with an old school friend and fellow runner Mike Deakin, for some time shared a flat in York Street, just off Friargate. I don't remember anything in the way of cooking or cleaning ever being on the agenda, but we had a good time along the lines of working hard and playing slightly harder, an easy excuse for holding too many parties. Of the three of us Vic was the true party animal and often arranged something without telling us, so from time to time 'Knocker' Deakin and I would turn up at the front door only to be refused admission to our own home by some total stranger 'because Vic's having a party'. It was perhaps as well for Deakin, who unlike me still felt he could make the very top as a runner, that Vic was never likely to stay in Derby long. He left after eighteen months or so and eventually moved into television, where he finished up a very big hitter indeed as head of Sky Sports, a role which has enabled him to wield huge influence. It was Vic, as one of Rupert Murdoch's right-hand men, who oversaw the massive deal with the Premiership and who took Test cricket away from terrestrial television. Quite a career. Over a relatively short time Derby produced an extraordinary number of journalists who went on to great things. David Mannion, a serious-minded young chap with a very good brain, became and still is ITN's editor in chief, and an old footballing pal Trevor East also made his way in commercial television. Trevor took a rather unconventional route, initially joining the team of *Tiswas*, a madcap Saturday morning show for children which frequently involved he and his colleagues being dumped in a bath of baked beans or having cold custard poured over their heads. It seemed right up Easty's street because there was a time when he seemed unwilling to take anything very seriously, but he decided on a change of direction and moved through the hierarchy quickly to become head of ITV Sport. It was fairly soon after East joined ITV that the company decided they wanted Brian Clough to do a regular Friday-night spot on their sport preview programme and on the basis that he and Brian were friends Trevor confidently volunteered to do the negotiating. Delighted when Clough immediately agreed to take the job, Eastie asked how much he wanted by way of payment. 'Hey Trevor, as much as possible,' responded Cloughie with a broad smile, firing the ball firmly back into the disconcerted East's court. East later joined BSkyB, was briefly a Derby County director and is now head of sport for Setanta, one of Europe's leading Pay-TV companies where he has succeeded in pinching the rights to some Premiership football matches from Sky – Sky's negotiations having been overseen by his old mate Vic Wakeling. Small world.

Mark Sharman, another product of that era, also made it to head of ITV sport, a position he still holds. Though obviously gifted and with something of the jack-the-lad about him, Mark seemed such an easygoing young man that I find it hard to visualise him now telling Gabby Logan and Steve Rider what to do. Joe Lovejoy, who I took on at Derby to report Notts County matches in the late 1960s, has progressed just a touch since then. He also works for Murdoch and now peers out at me every week from the pages of the *Sunday Times*, where he has been chief football writer for some years. Joe sported a fine bushy beard in his Derby days but perhaps felt a beard was in some way not compatible with his stature as a heavyweight Sunday paper journalist, as it has now disappeared. Mike Ingham, once of Radio Derby, currently does a superb job as a football commentator/reporter on Radio Five Live and another former colleague, Alan Hill, has also made his mark. Alan was never cut out for evening newspaper work, the discipline of deadlines, or even getting to work vaguely on time, but he was a superb writer and found his niche as a biographer of famous cricketers, a skill which I imagine has earned him a very comfortable living. However, there was no better writer than Mike Carey, whose job in the *Derby*

Telegraph sports department I took when he moved to the town's news agency. Carey produced reports of such consistent brilliance that he was appointed cricket correspondent to the *Daily Telegraph*, succeeding legendary figures like E. W. Swanton and Michael Melford and seemed destined for similar eminence, but his temperament let him down and he resigned after some inconsequential squabble with his office. Rather more successful in the long term was Lionel Pickering, who as a young man left the *Derby Telegraph* sports desk to try his luck in Australia. He returned with the idea of starting a free newspaper, a concept he had seen work effectively on his travels, but which was unknown in the UK and though he had no staff, no premises and nowhere to print the paper, told me he was confident he could make a go of it. I felt I should mention this to the *Telegraph*'s general manager Philip Ball, who was highly amused. 'Young Lionel? He's going to start his own paper and give it away for nothing?' and off he went chuckling and shaking his head. Three years later Lionel was living in a magnificent country house, gardens open to the public at weekends, his free newspaper the *Derby Trader* having revolutionised publishing in the UK. Soon the Trader group had spread throughout the Midlands and Lionel subsequently sold out for millions, enabling him to buy Derby County, the club he had supported since his school days. Sadly he died not long ago.

Probably the best known of all Derby journalists from what might almost be termed a golden age was Terry Lloyd, a charming man who was on his way to achieving legendary status when he was tragically and unforgivably killed by United States forces in Iraq in 2003. 'Terry Lloyd, News at Ten...' it was a sign-off that became familiar to millions of viewers. Terry's first ever on-camera interview was far from any war zone and one remembered fondly by those of us who were there. It took place on the Baseball Ground pitch one Friday with a very young Terry charged to chat with Brian Clough about the following day's match. It was a fairly straightforward assignment, but Terry was not surprisingly a bag of nerves and not helped by the fact that Clough was being driven to distraction by Peter Taylor shouting hilarious but needless advice to both of them from the touchline. They must have had at least a dozen false starts before finally completing an interview which, when shown that night, was cut to about twenty-five seconds. The death of Terry Lloyd at the peak of his powers stunned everybody who knew him, in part because fame had not changed him a jot. He remained a down-to-earth

Derby lad with no airs and graces, modest, funny and loyal to his old friends. Reading reports of the inquest into his death was heartbreaking. The Lloyd family was never far from tragedy. His father Aled, a police sergeant, had been killed in a car crash answering a 999 call and his actor brother Kevin, famous for playing Tosh in *The Bill*, had drunk himself to death before he was fifty. So much talent wasted.

CHAPTER 15

SORRY BRIAN – I'M WATCHING RUGBY

While football always dominated the sports pages of the *Derby Telegraph*, there was a life away from Derby County and it was a life that interested me, something which Brian Clough never began to understand. Why from time to time would I prefer to watch the national cross-country championship or a big local rugby match rather than take my usual seat in the Baseball Ground press box? It always amused Peter Taylor, who when a game against Liverpool or Manchester United was coming up might ask whether I was covering it or whether it clashed with the Spondon half-marathon or the Clay Cross swimming championships, but for some reason it seemed to irritate Brian, who clearly felt it was my duty to climb on to the Derby County bandwagon in August, fasten my seatbelt securely and not move again until May. Huge though my involvement was with football there was no way I could do that. Cricket, athletics, rugby, boxing, golf, cycling, rowing, I loved them all and far too often found myself involved almost with realising it. As a child, cricket had been as much a part of my life as football, probably a greater part, and that was never going to change as I grew older, but eventually I came to realise that trying to be sports editor while also covering Derby County and Derbyshire cricket was not very sensible, though I clung on to Derbyshire for as long as I could before handing the job over to David Moore. Covering cricket was a real pleasure, in part because most of the people involved were so nice. Those were the days, apparently now long gone, when players from both sides would often socialise from close of play until closing time and sometimes into the early hours of the morning. Sussex were especially good value and many were the catches dropped in the slips during the first hour of play after a long evening in the Bell Hotel. There were some memorable nights, notably when Colin Milburn, the mighty Northamptonshire batsman, had at least half a dozen goes at walking through the door of the Bell on his way to the gents before he actually made it. Derbyshire back then thrived as they had for years on the prowess of their fast bowlers; that and the brilliance of Bob Taylor, who so far as Derbyshire supporters were concerned was the best wicketkeeper in the world. Bob was a Fred Astaire among wicketkeepers, brilliant without apparent effort, modest and self-effacing when not in action. When I bumped into him before the start of play in a Test match in Cape Town not so long ago, it was the first time I had seen him for the best part of thirty years, but he was just the same delightful Bob, chatting away happily until he suddenly remembered he had seventy corporate guests to sort out and strolled off towards the pavilion.

On those cold early April days at the start of the season, the County Ground at Derby could be the most inhospitable cricket ground in the country, the wind whipping across from the east and no place to face bowlers like Les Jackson, Brian Jackson, Harold Rhodes and, later, Alan Ward and Mike Hendrick, but it was no place for fielding either. On one memorable occasion, while a handful of us huddled in the freezing, unheated press box, Tony Lewis led Glamorgan out on to field with a blanket round his shoulders, which he handed to a grateful-looking umpire. When play started the players, most wearing three sweaters and tracksuit bottoms under their flannels, waddled about like Michelin men until, some time before lunch, the people working the ancient mechanical scoreboard claimed it had frozen up and they could not continue. I don't think I have ever been colder at any sporting event and that includes standing on the touchline of Buxton Rugby Club's ground in the middle of January. These days, of course, mature trees provide a screen and the entire ground is almost unrecognisable; no Grandstand Hotel, no landlord Charles Townsend doing his chaotic best to run it and no Douglas Carr leaning on the bar laughing like a demented hyena. Major Carr, the Derbyshire secretary, was not everybody's cup of tea but I was one of those who thoroughly enjoyed his company and his often hilarious anecdotes, delivered in that wonderful cut-glass accent, about canvassing on behalf of the Conservative Party candidate in unlikely places like Allenton and Alvaston, where support for the Tories was traditionally rather thin on the ground. He was also a much better secretary than he was often given credit for. He did, after all, have to help steer the county through all the machinations of the Harold Rhodes 'throwing' affair. Rhodes was a very fine bowler whose career was wrecked by allegations that he threw. He was eventually cleared, but only after eight years of effort during which his chances of playing regular Test cricket disintegrated. Understandably he was often depressed and frustrated, though his teammates usually kept him smiling, not least by nicknaming him Percy after Percy Thrower, the television gardening personality of the time. There were jokers in the team like Mike Page, whose laid-back attitude wrecked any chance he had of fulfilling his potential. There were those who thought Page had England potential – Rhodes was one of them – but Mike could not apply himself. He was a superb close-to-the-wicket fielder and a batsman of genuine class, who was rarely bowled or lbw but got himself out through some silly lapse in concentration. It was noticeable that towards the end of the season, when contracts were coming up for negotiation, he suddenly started putting some decent scores together.

I followed boxing closely through the vintage years of the 1950s when Rocky Marciano was annihilating all before him and Sugar Ray Robinson was king of the middleweights. The sixties, of course, brought the young Cassius Clay and somewhat further down the scale, Derbyshire's own hero, Jack Bodell. By the time Jack had emerged as a genuine contender I was no longer reporting boxing, but I continued to go to Jack's fights if I could, because I had for some time been friendly with his manager George Biddles. I was introduced to Biddles by Arthur Musson, landlord of the Rose and Crown at Draycott and midland area secretary of the British Boxing Board of Control, who had taken me under his wing when I was a trainee. As a youngster I had been fasci-nated by famous boxing figures like Jack Solomons and Harry Levene, so welcomed the chance to get to know Biddles, who at that time was managing Hogan 'Kid' Bassey, the world featherweight champion. He was everybody's idea of the typical boxing manager, a clever wheeler-dealer with the engaging charm of somebody who would not harm a fly but might talk it into a fight with an angry spider if the money was right. Some saw him as a rather dodgy character, but Arthur Musson spoke well of him and Musson was for years one of the most highly regarded men in British boxing so that was good enough for me. Biddles did a great job with Jack Bodell, taking him to within one fight of a challenge for Muhammad Ali's world title. Jack was much too nice a man to be a fighter, but he boxed to the best of his modest ability and pulled off some brilliant and unexpected victories, most memorably when he out-pointed Joe Bugner for the British, European and Commonwealth titles at Wembley, a fight I watched from the ringside.

For fifteen exhausting rounds Bodell and Bugner effectively cancelled each other out. It was once rather unkindly said that Jack learned his footwork at a school for deep-sea divers and in truth Bugner was little better. They shoved and wrestled each other, threw numerous punches that didn't land, trod on each others toes, grappled on the ropes and generally drove the referee to distraction. It was a poor spectacle and by the end of the fifteenth round, when Jack was declared the win-ner, both men were absolutely out on their feet. I went off to the bar with the *Telegraph*'s boxing writer Jeff Petts and a few minutes later we were joined by Biddles, naturally delighted for Jack and at the thought of another good pay day for the two of them. We all had a celebratory drink. These days the winner of a Wembley title fight would be chauf-feured off to a top London hotel for the night, but this was 1971 and all of us had to get back to Derby that night, not least Jack, who was prob-ably due behind the counter of his butcher's shop the next morning. About three quarters of an hour later, when Jack joined us, showered and happy, but battered and obviously exhausted, we set off towards the car park. We must have been just a few feet away from the car when George took the keys out of his pocket, handed them to Jack and said, 'it's no good Jack, you'll have to drive. I'm absolutely shattered.' Not for the first time that evening, Jack took it on the chin. He drove back to Derby and dropped us all off before heading for his home in Swadlincote. What would Lennox Lewis have made of that, I wonder? In boxing terms that was as good as it got for Jack Bodell and to be fair to win three heavy-weight titles was some achievement, but what happened next was not so good. Biddles had guided his man very astutely, but the next step up was a big one, because in order to show he was worthy of a fight with Ali, Jack needed to prove himself against a genuinely world-class performer and the man chosen to provide that test was Jerry Quarrie. Biddles must have known he was taking a terrible gamble. Quarrie was widely rec-ognised as the best white heavyweight since Marciano and a man most tried to avoid at all costs, so the only upside of this contest was that if

Bodell was to win it would establish him at the very highest level. Sadly what followed was all too predictable. Those with blind faith in Jack travelled to London full of optimism, but Arthur Musson — at the ringside as timekeeper — was one of the many realists who feared the British champion had strayed out of his class. After just ninety-five seconds of the first round, Quarrie caught him so perfectly on the point of the jaw that the power of the punch lifted both Jack's feet off the floor. And that was the end of the fight. Musson summed it up perfectly a few minutes later when he said that in all his years in boxing it was the first time he had seen somebody unconscious going upwards. Quarrie, who can never have enjoyed an easier night's work, was asked later whether Jack had proved an awkward opponent, a fairly ludicrous question on the circumstances. 'Well,' he said, after some thought, 'he certainly fell awkwardly.' From then onwards it was downhill and Jack fought only twice more, eventually losing his three precious titles to Danny McAlinden at Villa Park. It was not a good night for boxing, because with Jack on the floor after being clobbered by a right cross, McAlinden's family and supporters started climbing into the ring and celebrating even though the count was still going on. It was all very unpleasant, but Jack did not even mention it when, an hour or so later, he announced his retirement to a handful of well-wishers and journalists, some of whom had supported him, others who had mocked his lack of style in the ring. He spoke almost eloquently about how much he had enjoyed his career and how proud he was of his achievements. Jack already had our admiration because he was such a decent man, but I think when he thanked everybody and shook hands so warmly with friends and critics alike, he went up still further in our estimation.

By now I had decided that covering Derby County on my own while at the same time trying to run the sport department was almost impossible. First I took on a young Londoner called Brian McDermott to help, then when he left turned to David Moore, a good footballer himself, who I had first met when he was playing for the Sheffield Press team against our Derby Pressmen. Dave stayed for some time — I was delighted to be best man when he married — but he then took something of a gamble by accepting Brian Clough's offer to join Derby County as programme editor. I'm sure the money was better, but football was an unpredictable game and what would happen if there was a regime change at the Baseball Ground? Later there was, of course, and Dave was left high and dry until he landed an excellent job with the *Daily Mirror*. Whether or not Cloughie lent a hand there I am not sure, but he would certainly have felt some sense of responsibility for David's plight and could have pulled a string or two, not that Moore was not perfectly capable of landing the job under his own steam. So into Dave's seat at the *Telegraph* came Gerald Mortimer and we tackled the Rams between us, an arrangement that seemed to work very well – and enabled me to sneak off when some other sporting attraction cropped up. Like a rugby match.

Derbyshire has never been a hotbed of rugby union, but the county produced some superb players in the 1960s and early '70s, most of them products of two good old-fashioned grammar schools, Lady Manners, Bakewell and Ernest Bailey in Matlock. As a result of this for a long time the two most successful clubs in the area were the two old boys' teams, the Mannerians and the Baileans, though it took a year or two and some heavy defeats before the more fashionable Derby and Chesterfield were prepared to recognise this. Lady Manners produced a remarkable string of outstanding players, some of whom were snapped up by the big boys. Terry Green was signed by Moseley, then a match for any team in the country while Tony 'Boney' Robinson and Jonty Pearce went to Nottingham, who back then played at a much higher level than they do now. All this was, of course, long before the days of professionalism otherwise others would have left, in search of fortune as much as fame. But players of the quality of Bob Winthrope and Trevor ('Charlie') Gratton happily stayed local, their only flirtation with top-class rugby being when they turned out for the Three Counties (Notts, Lincs and Derbyshire) in the County Championship. As a rugby man since my grammar school days this was right up my street and as I lived in Matlock became quite heavily involved with the Old Baileans, whose first team was perfectly described by the long-serving Derby Rugby Club stalwart Eddie Hilyer as an accident of birth. He could not have put it better. Unlike the Mannerians eight miles up the road, they also attracted incomers, the most influential of whom was John Lowry, a Leicester man who had been a student at Matlock Teacher Training College. Lowry was not only a very good player – a winger-turned-scrum half in Austin Healey fashion – but an outstanding captain and organiser and under his leadership Baileans gradually became one of the best junior sides in the country.

The team was built around a handful of extremely good players, of whom Dave Ramsden in the forwards and Wally Redfern at centre were especially influential. Ramsden could play prop, second row or No.8, but eventually settled in the front row where he became a regular for the Three Counties, a good ball player and as hard as nails. Redfern was in the David Duckham mould, a graceful runner with a wonderful outside break who always seemed to have time. All the team lacked was a top-class fly half and that problem was solved when the Baileans finally tempted Bob Winthrope down the road from Bakewell, a transfer which in local rugby terms was big news. The Baileans took off, embarking on a winning streak that lasted for the best part of two seasons, often running up 60 or 70 points against decent opposition and becoming the first and possibly only old boys team to reach the first round proper of the English Knock-out Cup. If only the league system had been in existence back then, but leagues were still years away and all Lowry could do was beg bigger clubs to give Baileans a fixture. More often than not he was banging his head against a brick wall built on good old rugby traditions of prejudice and snobbishness, because 'proper' rugby clubs did not demean themselves by playing old boys teams. However, the opportunity to make a point came at Ilkeston one Wednesday evening, when Derbyshire played Nottinghamshire, because the Derbyshire team contained eleven Baileans players, Redfern sadly not among them because of injury, while Nottinghamshire were represented by the bulk of the Nottingham club side. It was a walkover. Derbyshire won by 30-odd points to three, a margin which would certainly have been much greater had Redfern not been missing. The Nottinghamshire players, England full-back Dusty Hare and all, sat miserably in the corner of the clubhouse afterwards while Derbyshire supporters, most of them from Matlock, celebrated wildly. The ever-persistent Lowry had yet another go at the Nottingham club officials, but out of embarrassment or, more probably, sheer bloody-mindedness they still refused to offer even so much as a Second XV fixture. Ridiculous. It was a magnificent era, though there were occasional black days, the worst by far coming one cold Sunday, when Baileans were playing a Derbyshire Cup game at Buxton. They were cruising along 40 points in front when Redfern collided with an opposition centre and the crack could be heard on the touchline as this fine player's leg was smashed so badly that the bone was poking through his sock. By extreme good fortune the Buxton hooker was a doctor who had a medical bag in his car and, of course, knew what to do – otherwise heaven knows what might have happened. Andy Wood,

Wally's partner in the centre, was not the only player in tears and the game was immediately abandoned, Buxton conceding their place in the next round of the cup, though that was the last thing on anybody's mind at the time. Hindsight, of course, is infallible, but Baileans could easily have rested their best players because the following week they were due to play Birmingham Police in the first round of the English Cup, but that was not what happened in rugby in those days. I don't suppose it had crossed anybody's mind at the selection meeting that they could have put the second team out against Buxton and still won easily. Cloughie gave me his usual old-fashioned look and shook his head in a long-suffering sort of way when I told him a couple of days later I would not be covering the next Rams match because I was going to watch a junior game of rugby on the wide open spaces of Cromford Meadows with not a grandstand in sight, but so far as I was concerned it was no contest. The Baileans had rigged up a telephone line from pitchside to Redfern's home and gave him a running commentary throughout, a commentary which had a happy ending thanks to an inspirational performance by John Lowry. Sadly, Wally Redfern never played seriously again. I suppose it was very much in the nature of rugby that such a gifted player should have had his career ended in a fairly meaningless game on a tiny, wind-swept pitch in the middle of nowhere. Some months later, after a Three Counties game against Warwickshire at Coventry, a terribly posh chap wandered across and asked, 'How is your fellow Redfern? Far worse have played for England, you know.' Accident of birth? Had Wally Redfern been born a generation later, it would have been Bath and Bristol for him, not Buxton and Bakewell.

It is curious how some people can be hugely enthusiastic about one sport, maybe two, yet have absolutely no interest in any other. Games of skill, played to a high level, are almost mesmerising so far as I am concerned, be it Seve Ballesteros getting himself out of trouble, Viv Richards scoring a hundred or Bjorn Borg and John McEnroe battling out a Wimbledon final. Athletics, I would accept, is something quite different; no ball, no hand-eye coordination and no requirement for endless discussion about systems and tactics. It is either in your blood or it isn't and if it isn't then while you might appreciate the style and power of a Steve Ovett or Sally Gunnell, the sport would probably only grab your attention properly every four years when the Olympics came round. For me running has always been more way of life than hobby and really that

is the only way it can be. Why else, in my early twenties, would I sometimes run from my home in Matlock along the canal bank to Ambergate
then down the A6 to Derby and round the ring round to Normanton,
where running-mate George Cull would have a change of clothes for
me? About twenty-three miles I suppose. Mad? Well, some would say
so, but George must have been just as mad, because he would leave his
house the same time as I left mine and we would meet somewhere
around Belper and run to his place together. Back there we had a wash,
a cup of tea and a bowl of his sister's excellent stew then I would get the
bus to the railway station and catch the last train back to Matlock in time
for bed at about 10.30. Not mad, perhaps, but possibly mildly eccentric.
By the early 1970s I had long given up any hope of making the grade
as a top-level distance runner. I was not bad but there were many better and work meant I still had very few opportunities to race. Later I
decided that, while I could never contemplate giving up running, I could
serve Derby and County Athletic Club better as an administrator, so I
became club secretary and later still started coaching and acting as team
manager. We had some excellent runners, like Jeff Eley, Alan Domleo,
Harry Leeming and Kevin Hinton and at Sheffield the club regained the
English cross-country team title after a gap of many years. Still to arrive
on the scene were Nicky Lees and Chris Woodhouse, both of whom
were to become major figures on the UK scene. Lees was a precocious
youngster who dominated English Schools cross-country and went on
to win the National junior cross-country championship and set 10,000-
metre track times that only a couple of today's Britons can achieve. Nick
wanted to be a top marathon runner and made a brilliant debut on a
very tough Derby course running around two hours fifteen minutes,
but he was never quite the same again after that. He usually did his long
Sunday run with me and a handful of other reasonable club runners,
when he should probably have been on his own running much faster.
Woodhouse was a different animal entirely. He had never run seriously
as a youngster and came to the sport quite late, but as soon as he did so
it was obvious he had not only abundant talent but that essential ability
to tackle the hardest training session. His father, well-known local fruiter
Jack Woodhouse, was convinced he would eventually start beating Nick
Lees, something which struck me as highly unlikely because Lees was
exceptional, but beat him he did. Some may remember one of the early
London Marathons when Woodhouse was hired to act as pacemaker and

led until the halfway mark, when he was obliged by his contract to pull out though he looked very comfortable and perfectly capable of carrying on to the end. The BBC commentators, who back then recognised hardly anybody unless they were world renowned, had no idea who Chris was and ridiculed his efforts as he strode out in front of the field, something which annoyed him greatly when he heard about it later as well it might. It infuriated us back in Derby, too, because people paid to commentate should have been able to identify a man who was one of the country's best runners and had represented England many times. Derby did well as a club, but real success for me as coach and team manager was to come after the move to Wales. The Swansea Harriers team was another accident of birth and we travelled the country winning everything in sight, including twenty-one AAA championship gold medals in one twelve-month period. We went on to even better things, finishing second in the European club championship, in which we were beaten only by Sporting Lisbon, effectively the Portuguese national squad. Our spearhead was the brilliant Nigel Adams who was on the verge of greatness when his career was ended by a freak injury. Just a few months earlier he had won two AAA titles by a street and gone on to beat Olympic 10,000 metres and world cross-country champion Khalid Skah in a big race in China. He was a lovely man as well as being a wonderful runner and we were all devastated when he had to retire.

CHAPTER 16

PETER TAYLOR

If there was one thing that drove Brian Clough up the wall, it was reading or hearing that he was merely a front man and Peter Taylor was the real brains behind Derby County's success, and it was hard to blame him because this theory was quite common at one time, though mostly among those who had never met either of them and did not have a clue what was going on. But Taylor certainly played a massive role in Derby's success. He was acknowledged as a brilliant judge of a footballer, but there was far more to it than that. He knew Clough inside out, could predict his moods, encourage him and calm him. When Clough hesitated it was Taylor who nudged him forward, when Clough's impulsiveness bubbled over it was Taylor's restraining hand on his shoulder. Clough was not only a good judge of a player he was a shrewd judge of people and, though he would certainly never have admitted it back then, well aware of his own shortcomings, which is why he broke with tradition by appointing an assistant who was to all intents and purposes a partner. Of course there had been assistant managers before, but that is exactly what they were, assistants. Not Taylor. In fact, Peter was making a perfectly good job of managing Burton Albion when Clough, newly installed at Hartlepool, persuaded him to move to the north-east, a move he made without hesitation despite having to take a big drop in pay. It was a pivotal decision for both men and subsequently for Derby County and not just because of Taylor's remarkable ability to spot talented players. Peter could also sense an unhealthy atmosphere or potential flare-up and it was in those situations he was often at his best. The Taylor humour does

not translate well into the written word, he was just incredibly funny –
a sort of amalgam of Tommy Cooper, Les Dawson and Spike Milligan.
Almost everything was a corner-of-the-mouth aside, delivered with a
slight sideways tilt of the head. He never told jokes. He was just a natural
clown. One November Saturday in 1969 Derby went to London, played
very badly, and were walloped 4-0 by Arsenal. It was their heaviest defeat
since the great days had started and Clough was beside himself with
fury. The coach travelled back from Highbury to St Pancras Station in
stony silence, not even a newspaper rustling. Traditionally after a game
in London the players would have a quick beer in the station bar before
heading for the train, but this time Clough marched the entire party
– me included for some reason – straight through the doors of the Great
Northern Hotel and into a private room where everybody sat staring
into space. Peter glanced across at me, stuck his tongue in his cheek as
he often did and raised his eyebrows. A little later Clough got to his feet
and strode to the door, everybody following dutifully behind. Up to the
station we went, on to the train and into the reserved dining car, still
in silence. When was this going to end? As the train pulled out nobody
dared even pick up a menu, then Peter suddenly decided enough was
enough and when the steward appeared and started to walk through,
made some quiet aside to Clough that prompted a snort of involuntary
laughter. The ice had been broken and within five minutes the dining car was rocking as Peter took over, nobody more afflicted with the
giggles than Clough, who was wiping tears away as he ordered drinks.
The rest of the journey was a riot and back in Derby we piled into the
Midland Hotel for a couple of halves of Bass before all heading home.
The following Saturday normal service was resumed, the Rams playing
brilliantly when beating Sunderland 3-0.

That was Taylor at his best. Taylor at his most insensitive needed
Clough to rein him in and never more so than when Sunday morning
trials for youngsters were taking place. All football clubs get letters from
starry-eyed young hopefuls or their parents and most get the chance to
show what they can do, but unfortunately in many cases this does not
amount to very much. Thus it was quite common for Peter to watch no
more than five minutes of one of these games then turn to Brian, who
might be ten yards away and shout, 'Get 6 and 10 off, they can't play at
all' or 'Tell 4 and 7 to get changed. They've got no hope.' Clough was
appalled by this. He would stroll over to Peter, put a hand on his arm

and say, 'These kids are thirteen and fourteen years old. This is their big day. Do you want to break their hearts? We'll let them stay on until half-time.' Peter would shake his head, mutter to himself and draw heavily on the inevitable cigarette, but no matter how bad some of these lads were Brian would never let them be humiliated.

Clough and Taylor first met as players at Middlesbrough, where Clough was the fiery, high-profile goalscorer and Peter the largely unheralded goalkeeper and they quickly became good friends. Indeed, Peter always spoke of Clough as the first young player he identified as having star quality. Brian had turned up fresh out of the RAF to play in a Possibles *v.* Probables pre-season practice match:

> And it was obvious straight away that this was a lad who had all the instincts of a natural goalscorer. I told everybody in the club that this kid was going to be a great. I'm not sure they all agreed with me but I think his record proved me right.

Peter it was who encouraged the young Clough to be selfish around the penalty area ('all great strikers must have a selfish streak,' he used to insist) and Peter it was who Brian consulted when he was thinking about moving to Sunderland. Taylor was all in favour of that, but asked Brian to wait a few hours before signing. It emerged later that Peter wanted to place a large bet on Sunderland for promotion before the transfer was announced. Insider trading, I suppose. Peter was never one to miss a chance like that, but if betting was in his blood, football was his obsession. While Clough would often talk about family, holidays or politics, Peter talked of nothing but football, though he did once stop long enough to ask me whether I could fix his daughter Wendy up with a traineeship at the paper. This I duly did (thankfully she turned out to be very good) and Peter told me shortly after she started work that she had been befriended by Lucy Orgill, the paper's well-known women's page writer. 'We've checked her out,' he added, out of the corner of his mouth as usual. That was Peter. Had Wendy made friends with the Queen Mother Peter would have 'checked her out'. He was always checking people out.

It was as a talent spotter that Peter made his name and it was something he saw as a skill rather than a knack. He likened buying a player to buying a car or a washing machine:

You deal in hard facts and you must never back hunches. Watch a player in different conditions, not just at home, but in tough away matches when they will be under pressure. And you never ever bid for somebody on the basis of what they might do, always what you know they can do.

He also had little time for those in the game who so readily wrote players off. 'I've met scouts who have spent a lifetime telling managers that so and so is not good enough. What use is that? Show me somebody who is not afraid to back his judgement and say they've found somebody who is good enough.' Taylor certainly backed his own judgement. Once he went to the north-east to watch a lad who had been strongly recommended, but was unimpressed and wandered off to watch a game on another pitch. He came back with the signature of John Robson, a young wing half who made his Derby County debut at the age of seventeen and played right through the promotion and championship seasons. While at Hartlepool he spotted the young John McGovern in a trial game and was alleged to have said (and probably did), 'Lock the gates. Don't let him leave the ground until he's signed.' Young John, 'Border' to everybody, because the first winner he backed was called Border Flight, was still at school and a bright pupil, but Clough – given the job of winning over the headmaster – did his stuff as usual and John left school instead of staying on to do his A-levels. When they moved to Derby, Brian and Peter made signing McGovern one of their first jobs. I went down to watch him make his debut in the reserves and there was this skinny, waif-like figure wandering forlornly up and down the wing like a paperboy who had lost his bag. Years later, towards the end of a magnificent career, he was standing in Real Madrid's Bernabeu Stadium holding aloft the European Cup as skipper of Nottingham Forest. Taylor's sharp eye brought other good players to the club, usually for next to nothing. Football club scouts trawling non-League football were more often than not told to ignore anybody over eighteen, but that was never the Taylor way. He spotted Jeff Bourne playing for Linton United, a tiny junior club near Burton-on-Trent and Jimmy Walker swerving his way down the wing for Northwich Victoria in the Cheshire League. Bourne signed just before his twentieth birthday and Walker, who had probably long given up hope of a career in the professional game, when he was almost twenty-two. It was some time before Bourne made his mark, but Walker had an instant impact and played an important role in

Derby's promotion from the Second Division. Roger Davies was an even greater success. Peter was impressed when he first saw Roger playing for Southern League Worcester City and was soon back to have another look with Clough in tow. The chase for Davies had already started by then, because Torquay United had offered £3,000, a bid soon topped by Millwall and later Coventry City. Arsenal chief scout Gordon Clark then persuaded his club to go as high as £12,500 before Clough said he was prepared to pay £14,000. Worcester needed the money and their manager Wilf Grant was not only a friend of Taylor but also an admirer of Derby's emphasis on skill rather than brute force, so almost inevitably the deal went through. Though this was another feather in Taylor's cap, perhaps the real credit for Davies making the grade should go to Wilf Grant, who had spotted him as a gangling twenty-year-old centre forward playing as an amateur for Bridgnorth. As Grant paid just £100 for his man he could congratulate himself on a tidy profit. But Peter Taylor was not infallible. He had on his doorstep one of the best schoolboy players ever to come out of Derby, the brilliant Steve Powell, whose father Tommy had enjoyed a distinguished career with the Rams, yet he very nearly lost him and could not have complained had he done so. Powell was captain of England Boys, something which in itself should have aroused the interest of his home-town club, but for some reason Peter did not go to watch him. I among others nagged away to no avail but eventually, when his father told me Steve was thinking of joining Chelsea, I had yet another go at Peter and that did the trick. Clough's suggestion was not that they should watch Powell play at schoolboy level, but that he should go to the ground and play in a practice match. Back at the office, where Tommy worked in the *Telegraph*'s accounts department, I set this up and two or three days later fifteen-year-old Steve was pitting himself against the likes of Hector, Hinton and O'Hare. I was not there that morning, but evidently Powell was not only brilliant but was supposed to have barked 'leave it Terry,' to Terry Hennessey, as he steamed in for the ball, much to Hennessey's astonishment and Taylor's huge amusement. Hennessey was, after all, Derby's first £100,000 signing, one of the best players in the country and a Welsh international. Powell soon signed, but my strong impression was that Clough and Taylor fell out about this shambolic episode in quite a big way, Brian less than happy that such a talented lad had almost gone elsewhere. Peter really had no defence, but it was a rare blemish. As for Powell, he made his first-team debut at the age of just sixteen years and thirty days and a brilliant debut it was. He was astonishingly mature for such a young man.

Around this time Clough was looking for somebody to help develop a handful of young players in the reserves so I suggested Chris Barker, still turning out each week for Littleover Old Boys and running rings round defenders just as he had when we were young teenagers. I had mentioned him several times before, and though by this time Chris was in his late twenties and no longer a realistic candidate for League football, Peter thought he would go and have a look. To my surprise he was only moderately impressed, insisting that while Chris was a good strong player he was not as skilful as I had said. I was baffled, but all became clear when it turned out that Barker had missed the game Peter watched because of injury. I duly reported back that whoever he thought he was watching (presumably Chris Brown, a very good player at junior level) it was certainly not Chris Barker, but for whatever reason neither Brian nor Peter ever went for another look. This was a shame but at least in later years it gave Chris Barker a good after-dinner story.

Clubs did not look overseas for players in those days so it came quite out of the blue when Derby announced that a young black African player was arriving for a trial. I forget his name, which is hardly surprising since Peter immediately started referring to him as Jack White, but it created quite a stir because this was something unknown in English football. After a couple of training sessions he was chosen for a reserve game which drew quite a decent crowd and it soon became clear he had something. Though he was caught out by the pace and drifted in and out of the game, he was completely two-footed and insisted on taking corners on both sides of the field. He was very quick, had a ferocious shot and produced all manner of odd tricks with the ball – just the sort of things we see from so many African stars today. I suspect that were he to come on to the scene these days he would earn a decent living from football, certainly in a lower division, but even forward thinkers like Clough and Taylor could not quite come to terms with that particular sort of talent back then. The more outrageous the tricks this lad tried, the more hilarious Brian and Peter seemed to find it and when the trial period was over they duly dispatched him home without a second thought. Clough did not harbour an ounce of colour prejudice and I have no reason to think Taylor did either, it simply seemed the whole episode was something they could not take seriously, but at least it spared Peter the problem of having to master an unusual name. Peter always had trouble with people's names. Len Cantello, the West Bromwich Albion player, was variously Galento, Lentello and even Canaletto. Mike Summerbee at Manchester City was merged with his teammate Colin Bell to become Mike Summerbell, Derek Dougan occasionally morphed into Doug Deegan and the manager Colin Appleton might be Appleby, Appleson, Appleford or even Applewright, but never ever Appleton. When Derby made it into Europe he was little better with place names. Spartak Trnava in Czechoslovakia inevitably became Spartak Turnover, while the best he could make of Sarajevo was Sarajengo. But if he made mangling the English language an art form long before John Prescott came on the scene, he had no problem getting his message across where football was concerned. He detested Don Revie ('he couldn't lie straight in bed,' he so often said) – he was probably to some extent responsible for Clough's almost pathological dislike of the Leeds manager and his methods – and was cheerily dismissive of Joe Mercer ('great player, nice man. Much too nice to be a manager'). He was justifiably confident in his judgement of players, yet there was always a sense of insecurity lurking behind the easy laugh and the wisecrack. He was a heavy smoker and a serial worrier, especially when he felt directors were trying to get involved in football matters, and it was maybe no great surprise when he suffered a minor heart attack, though thankfully he was back at work fairly quickly. One thing for certain was that back in those Derby days Clough was very fond of him and owed him a great deal. There were some lovely moments. Peter, rarely far away from a racing paper, from time to time passed on strong tips to the dressing-room gamblers, which was handy because there was a betting shop close to the ground, but somehow Clough always got to know. One afternoon the small group of players who had slipped out to place a bet came back celebrating after the horse romped home, only to find a notice pinned to the dressing-room door: 'Any player visiting a betting shop wearing training gear will be fined one week's pay. Brian Clough'. Much mirth among the other players. Sometimes Brian was on the wrong end of the joke. He had always hated the thought of going to the dentist and with good cause because when he moved to Derby he had a set of rather ugly decayed teeth, so when told he should have them all removed he was a bag of nerves. He had been dreading this for weeks and insisted that Peter went with him for moral support and to drive him back to the ground. I was waiting there when they returned, Brian still very woozy from the effects of the general anaesthetic as Peter, holding by him the elbow, steered him into his office. 'Sorry, George,' said Peter as he walked in. 'I know what I promised but it didn't come off. I had three goes at pushing him under a bus, but one pulled up sharp and the other two swerved and missed him. We'll have to think of something else.' Brian gave him a big, gummy grin. That was how they were. At least back then.

CHAPTER 17

BRIAN CLOUGH

Brian Clough spoke often of his childhood and was absolutely devoted to his parents, who occasionally came down to watch matches at the Baseball Ground. His mother Sarah was a strong personality and, like her famous son, not to be trifled with. His father Joe was a little chap, rather shy, quietly spoken and rarely without his battered flat cap. They looked what they were, products of a tough upbringing in the industrial north-east and I remember Brian being outraged when, in his early days at Derby, he took them on holiday to an upmarket hotel in Devon where he encountered a rather unpleasant display of class prejudice. He was not then a familiar face to non-football followers and the manager of the hotel, who did not recognise him, took one look at Joe's flat cap and rather meek demeanour and immediately insisted they pay for their rooms in advance. After a brief conversation with Clough, very much of the one-way variety, he quickly changed his mind. Brian and his wife Barbara arrived in Derby with three children under the age of five, Simon, Nigel and Libby. Cloughie could be touchingly old-fashioned where his kids were concerned, forever fussing about quite trivial things, and even a few years later, could be heard shouting down the hall to Nigel, 'hey Igey I don't want you going out without your Balaclava on.' Poor Nigel must have been the only child in Britain in the early 1970s still wearing a Balaclava helmet. Brian was very much a children person. Not long after moving to Derby he hired a large minibus and took a group of underprivileged youngsters to Twycross Zoo for the day. I got wind of this and told him it would have made a great picture had he told us about it. This was not a good move on my part. For a moment I thought I was going to get the same treatment as the Devon hotel manager, but he just about kept himself in check. 'I didn't do it for publicity. I don't want people to think I would use kids that way. Please don't write a word about it,' he said, so I didn't and neither did I bother even to raise it with him when I later learned he had got into the habit of dropping off baskets of fruit at the Derbyshire Children's Hospital in North Street on his way home from the ground. Where children were concerned his emotions were never far below the surface. Once, at the Great Western Hotel next to Paddington Station, we were among a large group of guests watching the early-evening news in the television room when a particularly distressing report about the famine in Ethiopia was shown, illustrated by some heart-rending film of starving children close to death. There was much coughing and hard swallowing from this gathering of total strangers, silently watching these scenes of abject misery, but no such stiff-upper-lip inhibition from Brian. He sat there with tears rolling down his face saying 'terrible, terrible,' over and over again. That unusually open personality revealed itself in other ways, too. On a couple of occasions we drove past a wedding party arriving at a church and each time his reaction was identical and absolutely spontaneous. He pulled up, dashed across to the church and applauded for all he was worth as the bride emerged from the car and set nervously off, clutching her father's arm. He then strolled back to his car beaming broadly, got back behind the wheel and the conversation resumed exactly where it had left off. Curious, even slightly eccentric, but very much Clough.

We both lived in Darley Abbey, not 100 yards apart, so would occasionally share a car into town. One cold and miserable winter day we were heading along Duffield Road when Brian, having spotted an elderly couple waiting at a bus stop, stopped the car, established that they were off to do some shopping, and ushered them into the back seats. I thought he must know them, but obviously not. 'How are you?' (always with that long and heavy emphasis on the 'are'). The occasional yes or no floated through from the back as he interrogated them all the way down the centre of town: 'Have you lived round here long? Do you always get the bus or do you walk when it's nice? What are you getting, meat for Sunday? Do you like the Market Hall? Do you have beef? We like beef, mind you we like lamb as well. Do you like lamb? Make sure you chew it really well. Shouldn't you have a scarf on? You should buy one it's cold today.'

And so it went on until he pulled up by the Market Place and the bemused couple were deposited on the pavement. Not the sort of thing your average commuter does on his way into work, but Cloughie was not your average sort of person, although in many respects he conformed. If we stopped for fish and chips he did not march to the front of the queue; in the pub he waited his turn. What he might do – and frequently did – was pay for other people's supper, just as he would quietly pay for an old couple's groceries in the supermarket.

But neither did he get his reputation for swagger and conceit for nothing. He could be unbearably and embarrassingly rude, though there was little of that in his early days at Derby. At that time his noisy exuberance sat fairly happily alongside the good manners drilled into him by his parents, especially when in the company of women, but later, as his reputation and profile grew, he certainly changed. He was not, as some said, bombastic, because there was no high-handed haughtiness about him that I ever saw. Not for him the dreadful 'don't you know who I am?' form of pomposity (after all it would never have crossed his mind that there was anybody on the planet who did not know who he was), but he could be cruelly dismissive of people who were trying to do their best, often laying into them at the top of his voice and I suspect this got much worse when he was with Nottingham Forest. It was said Forest players would dive into doorways if they saw him walking down a corridor towards them, something I can never imagine happening at Derby.

He certainly did not manufacture an image for effect. Peter Taylor often spoke of a game at Charlton which Middlesbrough lost 4-3 despite Clough scoring a hat-trick. When the final whistle went and the players trooped into the dressing room, Brian tore off his boots, turned on his teammates and shouted, 'Maybe if I score four next week we might get a point.' No beating about the bush even then. No pretensions either, when he came into management. If he didn't know something he would ask, but anything he was certain about he was very, very certain about indeed. He was anything but impulsive, in fact he was usually extremely careful, especially where the players he had inherited were concerned. There were several he clearly didn't rate and others about whom he was initially unsure, notably Alan Durban. 'Durban? No, I'm not sure,' he said when I ran through the names of a few of his new staff with him. 'I don't think he's for me, but he's my best mate until I can get somebody better.' As it turned out he must have remained his best mate for some time, because it was five seasons before he did find anybody better. He moved Durban from inside right to right half ('It was either me or the groundsman,' said Alan after his first game in his new position, earning himself an instant fine which he later said was worth every penny) and the switch was an immediate success because 'Durb' went on to play a highly influential part in Derby's later triumphs and scored many crucial goals thanks to his knack of arriving late in the penalty area.

In those early days Brian often seemed the junior partner to the older and more experienced Taylor, from whom in football terms he had learned much of what he knew and on whom he had leaned heavily after suffering the injury that ended his career. He was almost deferential towards the great names in the game, so men like Bill Shankly, Harry Catterick and Bill Nicholson were always Mr Shankly, Mr Catterick and Mr Nicholson when he was chatting to them. It was also Mr Revie for a time, though not for long. As their paths crossed ever more frequently over the years, Clough developed a genuine hatred towards the Leeds manager. He regarded Don Revie as an out-and-out cheat who encouraged his players to cheat with him and to intimidate referees as well as opposition players. Brian once complained after an evening game at Elland Road that whenever Leeds had a corner or a free-kick in a dangerous position, a light would suddenly start flashing in the Derby goalkeeper's eyes. Far-fetched, perhaps, but he was convinced it was true. In some respects Revie and Leeds baffled him completely. 'They are a great team with great players, why do they have to do it?' he would ask. He was never happier than when his side beat Leeds; never more disappointed than when they lost to them. Why on earth he went there as manager I will never know because it was never going to work, as he should have known.

There has always been a strong fundamentalist streak within football. In recent years leading clubs have updated their attitude and approach to the game, but back in the sixties and seventies football people were stuck in a time warp and nobody more so than Brian Clough. Nothing could convince him that what had been good enough for him might not be right for the next generation of players. I was reminded of this when, late in the 1990s, the former Wales international Alan Curtis, then assistant manager of Swansea City, asked me for some help with training, 'because we train the players like we were trained and the people who trained us got us to do what they did when they were players.' In other words nothing had changed for generations. I was happy to help and recruited one of the Swansea Harriers, Shaun Tobin, to come down and train with the lads one morning. I got them all to run round the track for fifteen minutes, running thirty seconds as hard as they could, then jogging for thirty. In next to no time Shaun, in his middle thirties but very fit, had lapped them all and by the end of the fifteen minutes he had lapped some of these professional sportsmen three or four times. Once they had got their breath back the Swans lads were quick to point out that they were footballers not runners, but they had to admit that if they could get themselves as fit as Shaun (who meanwhile had gone for a ten-mile run), it could only help them on a Saturday afternoon. Cloughie would never have gone along with any of this. Throughout his time at Derby, he never accepted that there was any way of improving on the sort of training Wilf Mannion did at Middlesbrough and Len Shackleton at Sunderland. I argued time and again that they should do more endurance work and that if they were the fit sportsmen they were supposed to be they should be able to train twice a day at least three times a week. Brian waved all this away, even when I pointed out that when Manchester City won the First Division title their fitness advisor was Derek Ibbotson, the former world record holder for the mile. 'Look at John McGovern,' I would say. 'He runs himself into the ground every Saturday afternoon so in the last ten minutes he can hardly raise a gallop and starts losing tackles he would win in the first ten. That doesn't happen with Colin Bell [the Manchester City midfielder known as Arkle because if his stamina].' All I got was a patronising smile and a shake of the head.

He was just as set in his ways where diet was concerned. Every Saturday, dead on twelve o'clock, the players would sit down and eat a huge fillet steak, just as the previous generation had done and probably the one before that. So far as Brian was concerned steak was what footballers ate because it would help them play better when they kicked off three hours later and that was that. It was written in stone. Try telling Clough that all they would get was indigestion and back came the inevitable response – 'Steaks are good for you. I had steak. They have steak. Have a look at how many goals I scored and then tell me I was eating the wrong stuff.' It was pointless reminding him that not every player who enjoyed a medium-rare steak for lunch on a match day had quite as good a playing record as he did. Nor was it any use adding that other sports, especially athletics, had moved on long before and that most successful performers were eating pasta as part of carbohydrate packing as their big day approached. Pasta? You had that when you went to Italy for your holidays. His way of ending these conversations never changed: 'You stick to writing about it. I'll stick to managing.' He could always argue – and it was certainly a powerful argument – that his record at Derby justified his attitude towards training, diet and every other aspect of management, but he could not deny that when Arsenal stole a march on Derby and every other club by changing their pre-match eating habits as well as their training methods, thanks largely to the enlightened approach of goalkeeper Bob Wilson, they promptly did the League and cup double.

Surprisingly Brian was more receptive to information about players, happily acknowledging, unlike many in the game then and now, that the ability to recognise talent is not the sole preserve of former players. He would almost always listen to the views of experienced sports writers – especially those of his old mates from the north-east – though he once surprised me by showing no interest at all in a lad some of us had seen playing for Millwall called Keith Weller. I was not the only one urging Brian to watch him, but for some reason the shutters went down and it was always end of conversation when you got that old-fashioned look. Weller, of course, went on to enjoy a glittering career with Chelsea and Leicester City and to be fair to Brian, who never forgot anything, when Weller was chosen for England he was quick to say, 'You were right about him, weren't you?' He was also dismissive when I rang to tell him the Press Association had reported that Trevor Brooking had been transfer listed ('floats like a butterfly and stings like one too,' he once famously remarked of the West Ham man), but became extremely animated when I mentioned that my counterpart on the *Wolverhampton Express and Star* had told me Mike Bailey was one of his big admirers. I had no idea what Brian and Peter thought of Bailey but every time he had played against Derby he had been brilliant, dominating midfield completely, and nobody was very surprised when Wolves paid Charlton Athletic £40,000 for him in 1966. Urged by Clough to get Bailey's telephone number as quickly as possible – another illegal tapping obviously on the way – I duly did so, but never heard any more so obviously nothing came of this one. Brian was by then a great admirer of Alan Durban's midfield skills, but had Bailey been available that would surely have spelled the door for Alan.

Clough's uncomplicated approach to life ensured that while he clung firmly to some outdated ideas, he was equally loyal to the culture from which he and those ideas emerged. Nobody who knew him well would have been remotely surprised that he chose to march with striking miners in 1984. He would not bother to do that sort of thing for effect, because he had no need; he did it because he genuinely wanted to show his support for what he saw as a just fight. And yet he was impressed by authority and powerful people, especially powerful people with plenty of money. He enjoyed nothing more than rubbing shoulders with the famous, especially showbusiness types and big names from other sports like Geoffrey Boycott and the biggest name of all, Muhammad Ali, though he was less tolerant if they intruded into football. When TV reporter Gary Newbon was told by his bosses to get Cloughie to do a joint interview with Elton John, then chairman of Watford, he knew Brian would refuse and he was right, so the two men were duly put in adjoining rooms to be interviewed separately. Newbon realised Brian had taken pity on him when a head suddenly popped into the corridor and a voice said, 'Hey, come on then Gary. Get Yer Man in here.' Cloughie was fascinated by politics but not necessarily politicians and though he owned up to being a champagne socialist, something he could hardly deny in any case, he was very much to the left of the party. I never had the opportunity to ask him what he thought about New Labour, but it is easy to visualise him giving Tony Blair the mother and father of a dressing down had their paths ever crossed. However, for the most part if somebody was successful then that was good enough for Brian. When Ian Wooldridge, the *Daily Mail* sports writer, arranged to pay him a visit, Brian was so excited he rang David Cox, a local hotel owner, and asked him to deliver a case of champagne, which made a pleasant change after bottle after bottle of Blue Bass, the usual Baseball Ground tipple. In that sense he seemed to me far too easily impressed by fame and the trappings of wealth, which is probably why, when Derby County played in London, he had to try all the best hotels – the Savoy and Claridges were his favourites – though even when resident in these places he could only be himself. One morning we were all sweltering quietly in a stiflingly hot Savoy dining room when Brian strolled in for breakfast, stopped in his tracks, announced 'far too hot in here' and went round opening half the windows. Nobody else had said or done anything. That sort of confident approach was fine in situations like that, but his lack of tact (or plain bad manners) often did not endear him to foreigners. Having kept a bunch of reporters in Cologne waiting for ninety minutes while he finished a game of squash, Brian breezed into the room, turned to the German press and announced, 'It's no wonder you lot lost the war. My driver has just got lost in his own city for an hour and a half,' while in Athens, when asked why his players' win bonuses had been reduced, replied, 'So we can give the balance to the referee like you cheating bastards.' Not all his jokes went down well, though I'm not too sure the Athens comment was meant to be a joke. Paradoxically he hated bad manners in others, bad habits, too. Asked to present the annual Midlands' Young Player award to Trevor Francis he walked on the stage to find Francis standing with his hands in his pockets. His speech was short and to the point – 'Young man, you are very talented. Now get your hands out of your pockets and I'll give you this trophy.' Clough later made Francis Britain's first £1 million player and stuck him in Forest's third team. When he kept the wisecracks and occasional unwisecracks under control, a Clough interview made for riveting television. The big club bars were always noisy places on a Saturday lunchtime, but when from time to time they fell silent, a glance at the screen confirmed Brian was talking and inevitably providing good value. When it was put to him during one interview that he was earning twice as much as the Archbishop of Canterbury, he smiled broadly and replied, 'well all I can say is that the churches are empty every week and the Baseball Ground is full.' What better answer?

In *Clough the Autobiography*, ghosted by former *Sun* sports man John Sadler, Brian claims he was not especially motivated by money. John spent a lot of time at the Baseball Ground and knew Cloughie as well as I did, so he must have been laughing out loud as he wrote that. Yes, of course he was motivated by the need to be successful, but Brian was a football man through and through and football is an Arthur Daley sport in which everybody is motivated by money. Bungs? Back-handers? They were going on in the 1930s, so the likes of Sammy Crooks and Jack Bowers used to say, and nothing will have changed 100 years from now. One of the better-known Derby County stories concerned a transfer after which, legend has it, a girl cleaning the lounge of a hotel near Burton-on-Trent one morning found a bag containing thousands of pounds under the table at which Brian had been drinking the night before. She handed the bag to the hotel manager who put two and two together and rang the Baseball Ground to say, 'I think we have something of yours'. Nobody has ever categorically confirmed that this took place but when the story came to light I don't recall anybody disbelieving it. Why should they? In football anything goes. The saying 'there'll be a nice little drink in it for you' may not have originated in soccer, but there have been a good many nice little drinks over the years, the only real issue being how little is little. A glass of Scotch, John, or would you prefer a distillery?

Clough's loyalty to good friends was as legendary as his elephantine memory. He thought the world of that little group of sports writers from the north-east long after they could really be of any use to him and you did not need to know him for long to realise that once he trusted people that trust endured. He admired those he saw as good professionals and was a very close pal of the television commentator Brian Moore, who was a regular visitor to the Baseball Ground and later Forest. In the days before Sky introduced immediate after-match interviews, it was practically impossible to get a face-to-face chat with a manager until he had talked to his players, showered and changed, which could often be an hour or more. It was Brian Moore who thought he would try to introduce something fresh to ITV coverage by tackling a manager within minutes of the game finishing and it was Clough to whom he and his behind-the-scenes back-up man Steve Hamer put the idea. Brian, needless to say, was hugely attracted to the idea simply because it was something entirely new and yet another 'first' for him. 'Give me two minutes with the lads on the whistle then you come and fetch me,' he said, pointing to Hamer, who was to Moore and his colleagues roughly what Bill Frindall is to *Test Match Special* cricket commentators. Forest did not play well and when the final whistle went Clough was out of his seat in a flash and heading down the tunnel. Two or three minutes later, Hamer went to the Forest dressing room and as he arrived at the door heard Clough laying into the players for all he was worth. He knocked somewhat hesitantly and a few seconds later the door was flung open by a furious Clough to reveal Peter Shilton, Larry Lloyd, Kenny Burns and company sitting hunched on a bench like St Paul's choirboys being told off for singing out of tune. He looked at Hamer, there was a second's silence, then, 'I'll be with you in ten seconds... and [turning to the players] you lot don't move.' The door slammed and he strode off down the corridor to do the interview. 'You lot' almost certainly didn't move.

Brian Moore often saw the curiously whimsical way Clough's mind worked, too. He, fellow commentator Martin Tyler and Hamer were having a cup of tea with Brian after Forest had played at West Ham, a game in which Forest's Lee Chapman had not played very well, when Cloughie suddenly asked, 'How many VCs were awarded in the last world war do you reckon?' Not surprisingly they had no idea. 'I don't know,' said Moore. 'Two or three? Five? Maybe more.' 'Well however many it was I deserve them all for keeping that bloody man Lee Chapman on the field for ninety minutes,' said Clough. There was a further pause, then he turned to Moore again – 'You look tired, Brian, have a good fortnight's holiday as soon as the season ends,' then, warming to the theme, 'You, Martin, you should have a long weekend and you, Hamer, you don't deserve a holiday at all.' As the TV men reacted with roars of laughter, Cloughie resumed sipping his tea, not quite sure what it was they found so amusing. When Moore died after a long period of heart trouble Brian was by then very ill himself, but he was absolutely determined to make the long journey to Kent for the funeral of a man he genuinely respected, and duly did so. A friendship was for life, with one very notable exception. In the thirty-five or more years I knew him, I can recall Cloughie falling out seriously with only one friend and that was the biggest and closest pal of all, Peter Taylor. Brian claimed in his book that it was all down to one specific event when Taylor, by then managing Derby, signed John Robertson from Forest without even letting him know. Well, it's easy to understand that Clough would have been furious and disappointed at the time, but was it really something which would abruptly end such a close and successful friendship? It may have been a final straw, but the writing had been on the wall for some time. They were like a couple who slowly fall out of love almost without realising it.

So was Brian Clough the best manager of them all? Many good judges in and out of the game would say he was, indeed Martin O'Neill said so quite recently, emphasising that this was not just because of what he achieved but where and how he did it, which is a very compelling argument. Just two managers in the history of English football have won the First Division title with two clubs, Herbert Chapman (Arsenal and Huddersfield Town) and Clough, but what made Clough's achievement unique was that he had first to lift both Derby County and Nottingham Forest from the depths of the old Second Division. To some Clough was a loudmouth and a bighead who simply got lucky. Well, he was certainly loud and he didn't deal in self-doubt, but luck did not come into it. Look at his record and it is clear that nobody could be that lucky. Those who knew him very well would almost certainly agree that the cruelly premature end to his extraordinary playing career was what made him so relentless in his desire for managerial success. When he collided with Bury goalkeeper Chris Harker on Boxing Day 1961, doing irreparable damage to his right knee, he had a goalscoring record that nobody had approached nor ever would: 251 goals in 271 matches. He was only twenty-six when he was injured so if he felt both cheated and determined to seek fulfilment in management, who could blame him? Pure strength of personality played a huge part in that success, but especially so in his early days at Derby before he had truly made his reputation. When he arrived he had an aura to which people immediately responded, one of those who attract glances wherever they go, and he was always impressively positive. Indeed he was never one for reminiscing about his own career and was sometimes quite vague about matches he had played and goals he had scored. When I told him I was moving to Swansea he said he could not remember whether he had ever played there, so I checked the records and it turned out he had done so twice, first for Middlesbrough and then the following season for Sunderland. He scored four times in the first game and got a hat-trick in the second. Seven goals in two games and he couldn't remember. Or so he said.

Some current football writers, most of whom were not around when Clough was casting his spell over English football, refer constantly to his great motivational powers, as if motivation alone was the reason for his success. Of course it played a part, but a relatively small one. His great skill, in tandem with Peter Taylor, was in judging talent and creating teams which best utilised the players at his disposal, something no England manager has done since Alf Ramsey. Brian has often been described as the best manager England never had which may or may not have been the case. We can be sure, however, that had he been given the job after the Don Revie fiasco he would always have known his best team and never have tinkered with systems in the run-up to a game. Those who worked closely with him might sometimes have raised an eyebrow at some of his methods, but they would certainly agree that he was remarkably good at getting the best out of people and that certainly was where he came into his own as a motivator. As Willie Carlin once said, 'You might occasionally want to thump him, but you would give him your last half dollar.' While it seems his man-management skills deteriorated towards the end of his time at Forest (and were never seen at all during the Leeds United debacle), his handling of players at Derby was instinctively deft and often inspired. Carlin recalls a spell when his form deserted him completely:

The harder I tried the worse I got and it turned into an absolute night-mare. Every Monday we had a lengthy meeting about the previous Saturday's game and I would sit there in the dressing room waiting for him to launch into me, but he never did. Then gradually my form came back and I finally had a half-decent game. We had the usual Monday meeting and he said nothing to me at all, until we all got up to go, then he turned, looked me in the eye and said 'And it's nice to see you earning your money again.' Brilliant. I never looked back after that.

That ability to get the best out of players manifested itself in all sorts of odd ways. Alan Hinton, always with an eye for business, was once sorting out some sort of deal on a match day when he realised he was running a touch late and dashed into the dressing room about two minutes after the deadline to be met by a less-than-thrilled manager.

'Sorry, boss, I…'

'Ten pounds.'

'But boss, I just…'

'Twenty pounds.'

'Boss, I only…'

'Thirty pounds.'

When it got to £40, Hinton decided to admit defeat and sank into a corner, while those out of Clough's line of vision rocked with silent laughter. Inevitably Hinton, totally wound up, went out and played a blinder. As Cloughie doubtless knew he would.

CHAPTER 18

AND SO TO SWANSEA

A famous Welshman, once asked whether there was a word in the Welsh language which equated to the Spanish *mañana*, apparently thought for a second or two before concluding there were several, but none which conveyed quite the same sense of urgency. A little unkind, perhaps, but it is certainly easy to be seduced by the gentle pace of life in Swansea, not for nothing known as the graveyard of ambition and littered with people who arrived as young high-fliers, put down roots and refused to move away. Quite what Brian Clough would have made of it had he taken up an offer to become manager of the Wales football team is anybody's guess, but his knowledge of the country's geography was certainly a bit sketchy. I had not been in Swansea long when he telephoned with a surprise invitation.

'We're down your way in the League Cup in a couple of weeks, do you fancy it?'

'Are you? I didn't realise that.'

'Yes, Chester – that's somewhere near Wales isn't it?'

'Well it is, yes,' I said, 'but why not invite me to the home leg, it would be easier to get to?'

'OK, up to you,' he replied and the phone went dead. Yes, we're all fine Brian, thanks for asking.

I saw Cloughie from time to time but inevitably trips back to Derby became less frequent as the years went by. His occasional telephone calls more or less dried up and when I saw him on television and read of his increasingly eccentric behaviour it was easy to see what was happening.

The restless, urgent man I remembered, fit and bouncing with energy, was turning into an unhealthy, bloated, erratic shambles and it was sad to see. Friends would ring or write to say how difficult and increasingly unpredictable he had become as his health deteriorated, though that was plainly evident from 200 miles away. Having turned down editorships at Torquay, Exeter and Chelmsford (graveyard of ambition?), I eventually took charge in Swansea and enjoyed several years looking after the *Evening Post*. Newspaper editors, even out in the sticks, are fortunate to have an interesting and varied life simply by the nature of their job. Visits to Downing Street and the Foreign Office, tea with the Queen ('I'm not really sure Mr Beckham should be driving his car with his foot in plaster,' she remarked before the 2002 World Cup finals), visits to the European Parliament, lunch with the Emperor of Japan, invitations to big sporting events – they came and went and it was easy to become blasé about them. News events stick more vividly in the memory, most obviously the Twin Towers catastrophe in New York and the death of Princess Diana, yet the most subdued atmosphere in the newsroom I remember came on the day a madman mowed down a class of tiny school children in Dunblane. As the death toll rose the room became quieter and quieter and when a class photograph of these little tots arrived, the heads of those who had died neatly circled, there was a good deal of blinking and hard swallowing, especially among those who had small children of their own. It was a horrible day, one which took me back many years. It is commonly said that all older people remember where they were and what they were doing when they heard President Kennedy was killed. The same could surely be said of the Aberfan disaster, when an entire school in South Wales was wiped out, and the only occasion I can remember when some television reporters cried openly as they tried to tell us what was happening. Thankfully such events are few and far between.

Out of the blue came a wonderful invitation when my old pal Steve Hamer, by now a director of the National Sporting Club at the Café Royal in London, rang to see whether I would like to be a surprise guest at a tribute lunch for Cloughie. It was a great occasion and a reminder of just what a remarkably dominant personality he remained, ill though he was by then. 'There's an old friend to see you, Brian,' said Hamer, keeping me out of sight, directly behind him. As Steve stepped to one side, Brian glanced up, struggled from his chair and suddenly I was enveloped in a huge bear hug, his right hand slapping over and over again into the middle of my back for the best part of half a minute. 'We worked together in Derby,' he said by way of explanation to those who had watched all this going on, before plonking back into his seat, sitting me next to him and insisting on holding my hand for the next ten minutes. Typical emotional Clough and, I have to admit, a bit of a choker. Ronnie Fenton, one-time assistant manager at Forest, was effectively Brian's minder by this time, his primary job being to ensure he stayed off the alcohol as much as possible when he was on public display and he did a brilliant job that day. Though he didn't stint on the sherry or the wine, Brian was still in fine form after lunch when he joined the then Charlton manager Alan Curbishley and former Conservative cabinet minister David Mellor for a question-and-answer session chaired by BBC commentator John Motson. Clough, never much of a lover of Tory politicians, reduced Mellor to something of a gibbering wreck, revealing a surprising knowledge of the Thatcher government's neglect of investment in sport, while Curbishley kept a sensibly low profile and Motson struggled to exert some sort of control. The guests, most of them young businessmen, enjoyed this hugely, though some betrayed their youth and unfamiliarity with the Clough era.

'How is Peter Taylor these days?' asked one young chap.

'Not very good,' said Cloughie. 'He died years ago you daft bugger.'

Another questioner was a bit more knowledgeable. 'Didn't a bent referee cost you the European Cup one year?' he asked.

'Well, he cost us a game in Europe, yes. We got knocked out,' said Clough. 'Bloody disgrace.'

'But didn't it end in tragedy? Didn't the ref get knocked over and killed by a car?'

'Tragedy? The only tragedy was that I wasn't driving the f——ing car,' replied Brian triumphantly, revelling in the roar of laughter that followed what was, for better or worse, a piece of vintage Clough.

Obviously I did not realise at the time that this was to be the last time I would see him, but if there had to be a last time, then it could not have been bettered. Three years or so later I was having a quiet beer in my local when a friend walked in. 'Sorry to hear about Cloughie,' he said as he ordered himself a drink, a remark that could mean only one thing and I was astonished how affected I was as countless memories flooded back of an era unmatched in Derby County's history. What luck to have been part of it. Right place, right time. Brian's memorial service at Pride

Park was a magnificent occasion. The best part of 12,000 people turned out on a filthy night, many from Nottingham, as the traditional enmity between the two sets of supporters was set to one side. They heard a superb address by Martin O'Neill and witnessed an extraordinary display of sheer willpower by Brian's widow Barbara when she read a long and highly emotional poem written by a fan about 'Cloughie and the famous green sweatshirt'. While some were reduced to tears, Barbara didn't lose her composure for a second, striding off the pitch at the end with the bravest of smiles. But it was son Nigel who had the last word as a huge clap of thunder broke over the ground as he was paying his own tribute to his father. 'That's Dad rearranging the furniture,' he said. Or almost the last word. Somebody had done a lot of research and eventually found a tiny piece of TV film that fitted the occasion. As we all stood to leave the ground, that famous face filled the giant screen in the centre of the pitch and from the speaker system a familiar voice boomed 'Hey. And thank you very much for coming.' It was lump-in-the-throat stuff.

THE LAST FEW years before my retirement were hugely enjoyable as the *Evening Post* flourished thanks to a very talented staff. Great fun though it was, after forty-four years chasing fire engines and football managers my thoughts started to turn life after newspapers. I agreed to stay on for a few months longer than necessary, spending a good deal of that time planning trips to watch England play cricket and then it was time to go. I was given a marvellous farewell lunch, attended by the local great and good, from the Lord Lieutenant to British Lions rugby star Robert Jones, cabinet minister Peter Hain, my old Derby County pal Alan Durban and the singer Bonnie Tyler. There was a message from the Cloughs, too. It was memorable day for me, all rounded off by the wonderful Morriston Orpheus Choir who upstaged everybody.

And that was it. Off home, still not very neat with ink, but with a million happy memories.

INDEX

If you are interested in purchasing other books published by The History Press, or in
case you have difficulty finding any of our books in your local bookshop, you can also
place orders directly through The History Press website

www.thehistorypress.co.uk